CONFLICT AND CONSENSUS
IN THE AMERICAN REVOLUTION

BASIC CONCEPTS IN HISTORY AND SOCIAL SCIENCE

Conflict and Consensus in the American Revolution

Edwin C. Rozwenc, Ph.D.

Chairman, Department of American Studies
Amherst College

Donald P. Schultz, M.S.

Chairman, Department of History
Ann Arbor High School, Ann Arbor, Michigan

 D. C. HEATH AND COMPANY

BOSTON • ENGLEWOOD • INDIANAPOLIS • SAN FRANCISCO

ATLANTA • DALLAS

TABLE OF CONTENTS

CONFLICT AND CONSENSUS
IN THE AMERICAN REVOLUTION

A LITTLE more than a dozen years ago, the president of the American Sociological Society announced that a study of the problems of consensus was the most important way to understand the behavior of men. "I regard the study of consensus" Professor Louis Wirth declared, "as the central task of sociology which is to understand the behavior of men in so far as that behavior is influenced by group life."

Why should the study of consensus appear to be so essential to one of our leading social scientists? For most of us, the word "consensus" has been a word of common use in the English language for hundreds of years. Most often we use it to indicate that there is an agreement or a common accord among the members of a committee, or among the people in a public meeting, or among the members of any political or social group that has to make decisions.

In the thinking of many social scientists, however, the concept of consensus is not exactly equivalent to the idea of agreement in the ordinary sense. They believe that the quality of agreement reached in a consensus is different from more usual forms of agreement. Consensus, they would argue, is not the same thing as a majority opinion. It has to be an agreement that includes more than a mere

Part 1

The Concept of Consensus

majority in any group or society; and it is not necessarily expressed in the immediate decisions of the majority.

This difference between a mere majority decision and a consensus becomes clearer if we think of some fairly obvious examples in American politics. For instance, the election of President Kennedy by a narrow majority in 1960 should not be taken as evidence that the American consensus includes all of the assumptions of "the New Frontier." Indeed, the consensus of the American people may be opposed to the large spending and unbalanced budgets which are necessary to carry out the New Frontier program. Or, to use a different type of example, there may be an overwhelming consensus of the American people in favor of federal aid to education, but both houses of Congress, for various and complex reasons, seem to express a majority decision against such a measure.

Thus, consensus is a deeper and more stable kind of agreement than that which is expressed in the day-to-day decisions of the President or Congress, even in a representative democracy such as ours. The quality of the agreement that is expressed by this concept of consensus is very close to the kind of agreement that we think of when we use the word "custom." R. E. Park and E. W. Burgess in their *Introduction to the Science of Sociology* (1924) defined the concept of consensus in these explicit terms: "The continuity and life of a society depend upon its success in transmitting from one generation to the next its folkways, mores, techniques and ideals. From the standpoint of collective behavior, these cultural traits may be reduced to the one term, 'consensus'."

Nevertheless, we must not reduce the concept of consensus to a neat formula too quickly. In particular, we must not assume that consensus is something that is diametrically opposed to conflict. A consensus is not simply a social glacier made up of frozen habits and customs; a consensus, particularly in modern democratic societies, may also be reshaped through political and social conflict. To be sure, it may seem disturbing and contradictory to say that consensus may be expressed through conflict. That is almost like saying the blackness of something black is expressed by its relationship to the whiteness of something white. But to anyone who has painted pictures, such an idea is not necessarily silly or contradictory.

Indeed, there are many situations in our everyday experience which illustrate this relationship between conflict and consensus. The game of football, for example, is a conflict situation of great intensity. Two teams of eleven players are engaged in a fierce and often bitter competition to see who can win the victory by scoring more touchdowns. Bones may be broken, blood may flow, and sometimes a player is killed on the field. Yet the football game operates with a highly developed consensus. There is an agreement to abide by certain rules and to accept certain penalties whether your team is winning or losing. The players on the opposing teams use the same fundamental techniques of running, kicking, passing and blocking. Moreover, the players of both teams share certain attitudes toward the game which leads them to play despite physical hazards. They may share a belief in the value of competition, of ruggedness; they may share the same desires for the elation of victory or the psychological lift of personal glory. Furthermore, the controlled conflict of a football game probably expresses some of the basic values of the *American* consensus — competition, teamwork, sportsmanship, and physical vigor.

In a similar fashion, political conflict in a democratic society like that of America can be a beneficial means of modifying and maintaining national cohesion and a national consensus. Political conflict may be a means by which the diverse groups of a complex democratic society can talk out their differences and arrive at day-to-day agreements and compromises which may eventually modify and reshape the slowly developing habits and attitudes that compose a consensus.

Such conflicts have reshaped many aspects of the American consensus in our history. By means of such conflicts between management and labor, we have been able to move from patterns of violence, boycott, and blacklisting toward a consensus that favors the more orderly processes of collective bargaining. In addition we have been able to move from established habits of discrimination against immigrant groups and Negroes toward a greater degree of equality of civil rights and a greater degree of equality of economic opportunity. Indeed, the struggles over civil rights for Negroes and other minority groups also represents an attempt to renew American ideas of equal rights and equal opportunity that are as old as the Declaration of Independence.

But political conflict does not always readjust the habits and attitudes that make up a consensus. Whenever political conflicts reach a point at which the contending parties no longer share basic values and attitudes, then a revolution or civil war is likely to tear apart the political and social structure of the nation. The American Civil War resulted when the contending parties in the North and the South reached such a point of intense disagreement.

Hence, by using the concept of consensus, we can find new ways to understand many important developments in American history. In particular, we can understand more clearly the nature of the American Revolution. It was by means of the American Revolution that we became an independent nation and, if we analyze the ideas and behavior of Americans during that Revolutionary generation, we can discover a great deal about the shaping of the American consensus.

In order to study the American Revolution in this way, we shall not be concerned so much with the causes of the Revolution as we shall be with the process by which an independent nation was organized. We shall focus our attention on the political institutions which Americans constructed during the Revolutionary era, on the social habits they fostered, and on the political ideas and attitudes they encouraged.

The American Revolution was not only a great period of institution-making, it was also a time of intense political conflict — a conflict *within* the Patriot party as well as *between* Patriots and

Tories. During the years between 1776 and 1783, eleven of the thirteen states adopted newly written constitutions. New governments were organized with changes in qualifications for suffrage and officeholding. New adjustments were also made in the relationship of executive and legislative power in these state constitutions. At the same time, important changes were made in law and in custom. In Virginia and the southern states, the state-supported Anglican church was disestablished. Virginia and other states also changed the laws of inheritance so as to eliminate the aristocratic devices of primogeniture and entail which were designed to perpetuate large aristocratic landholdings in the hands of the eldest sons. Massachusetts abolished slavery and other northern states provided for the gradual abolition of slavery. Most of the states, moreover, confiscated the landed estates of Tories and distributed them at attractive prices to all comers. Such changes could not be accomplished without considerable social strain and the Revolutionary period is full of intense political conflicts in the states and in the Continental Congress.

The main problem of this volume, then, is to investigate the relationship between conflict and consensus in the American Revolution. Was the American Revolution primarily a colonial rebellion in which the main issue was to gain independence from England? Or was it an internal revolution as well in which farmers, artisans, and small tradesmen battled for their democratic aspirations against entrenched local aristocracies? Did the political conflicts among Americans during the Revolution re-enforce a conservative consensus, or did they compel the shaping of a new American consensus?

To help us answer these questions, this volume contains various declarations and provisions taken from the laws and constitutions of the Revolutionary period as well as statements made by some of the influential leaders at that time. Some of these documents emphasize those considerations which united the American people in their common cause — hence, we can say that they use a vocabulary of consensus. Other documents stress points of controversy and dispute which divided Americans even while they were fighting for independence. To help us decide how we should explain the relationship between conflict and consensus in the American Revolution, we shall also read some interpretations of the American Revolution made by leading historians in the twentieth century.

When we remember that the American Revolution is the time of birth for the American nation, we can see that the study of consensus and conflict in the American Revolution may lead us to a better understanding of our society. America, to be sure, is a complex and rapidly changing society, but even a dynamic society retains many habits and attitudes that were developed in the historical past. In pursuing the questions raised in this volume, we can discover the sources of those ideas and values that we still cherish as part of our twentieth century American consensus.

Our first step in analyzing the relationship of conflict and consensus in the American Revolution will be to examine four significant documents by means of which the American people were being rallied in support of a common destiny, a common political philosophy, and a common definition of individual rights. These documents cannot tell us all that we need to know about the common aspirations of the Americans who supported the Revolution, but they are important examples of the ideas which were expressed not only in public declarations, but also in the written constitutions of the period. By studying these documents, we will be able to discover the ideas and values of Americans in the Revolutionary generation when they were trying to express their agreement about the proper basis for government, the rights of man, and the particular liberties which deserved special guarantees in the written constitutions. And since these documents were prepared primarily to unite Americans and to win their consent for the institutions of a newborn nation, we shall accept them as representative examples of the way in which the Revolutionary generation used a vocabulary of consensus.

Part 2

The Vocabulary of Consensus

1. THOMAS PAINE: "Common Sense" *

In the political crisis which followed the Boston Tea Party and the first armed skirmishes between American and British troops at Lexington and Concord, Americans hesitated as they attempted to choose between a policy of reconciliation with Great Britain, or a policy of independence. Thomas Paine, more than any other single individual, crystallized the feelings of Americans in favor of independence by means of his famous pamphlet, Common Sense. *This pamphlet, which was published early in 1776, quickly sold 150,000 copies, an amount most unusual for that time.* Common Sense *helped to clarify the debates about the merits of independence and, in July of 1776, the fateful decision was made to declare the independence of the United States of America. Read the following selection from* Common Sense *with great care and try to answer the following questions:*

1. Why does Paine think that independence for America is the only natural and reasonable course of action?
2. What kind of charter, or constitution, does he propose for the independent United States; what specific guarantees should this charter contain?
3. What do you think that Paine means when he says "the law ought to be king"?

I is repugnant to reason, to the universal order of things, to all examples from former ages, to suppose that this Continent can long remain subject to any external power. The most sanguine in Britain doth not think so. The utmost stretch of human wisdom cannot, at this time, compass a plan, short of separation, which can promise the continent even a year's security. Reconciliation is *now* a fallacious dream. Nature hath deserted the connection, and art cannot supply her place. For, as Milton wisely expresses,

° From Moncure D. Conway (ed.), *The Writings of Thomas Paine* (New York, 1894), Vol. I, pp. 91–92, 97–99, abridged.

"never can true reconcilement grow where wounds of deadly hate have pierced so deep" . . .

As to government matters, 'tis not in the power of Britain to do this continent justice: the business of it will soon be too weighty and intricate to be managed with any tolerable degree of convenience, by a power so distant from us, and so very ignorant of us; for if they cannot conquer us, they cannot govern us. To be always running three or four thousand miles with a tale or a petition, waiting four or five months for an answer, which, when obtained, requires five or six more to explain it in, will in a few years be looked upon as folly and childishness. There was a time when it was proper, and there is a proper time for it to cease.

Small islands not capable of protecting themselves are the proper objects for government to take under their care; but there is something absurd, in supposing a Continent to be perpetually governed by an island. In no instance hath nature made the satellite larger than its primary planet; and as England and America, with respect to each other, reverse the common order of nature, it is evident that they belong to different systems. England to Europe: America to itself. . . .

If there is any true cause of fear respecting independence, it is because no plan is yet laid down. Men do not see their way out. Wherefore, as an opening into that business I offer the following hints; at the same time modestly affirming, that I have no other opinion of them myself, than that they may be the means of giving rise to something better. Could the straggling thoughts of individuals be collected, they would frequently form materials for wise and able men to improve into useful matter. . . .

But as there is a peculiar delicacy from whom, or in what manner this business must first arise, and as it seems most agreeable and consistent that it should come from some intermediate body between the governed and the governors, that is, between the Congress and the People, let a Continental Conference be held in the following manner, and for the following purpose:

A Committee of twenty six members of congress, *viz.* Two for each Colony. Two Members from each House of Assembly, or Provincial Convention; and five Representatives of the people at large, to be chosen in the capital city or town of each Province, for, and in behalf of the whole Province, by as many qualified voters as shall think proper to attend from all parts of the Province for that purpose; or, if more convenient, the Representatives may be chosen in two or three of the most populous parts thereof. In this conference, thus assembled, will be united the two grand principles of business, *knowledge* and *power*. The Members of Congress, Assemblies, or Conventions, by having had experience in national concerns, will be able and useful counsellors, and the whole, being impowered by the people, will have a truly legal authority.

The conferring members being met, let their business be to frame a Continental Charter, or Charter of the United Colonies; (answering to what is called the Magna Charta of England) fixing the number and manner of choosing Members of Congress, Members of Assembly, with their date of sitting; and drawing the line of business and jurisdiction between them: Always remembering, that our strength is Continental, not Provincial. Securing freedom and property to all men, and above all things, the free exercise of religion, according to the dictates of conscience; with such other matter as it is necessary for a charter to contain. Immediately after which, the said conference to dissolve, and the bodies which shall be chosen conformable to the said charter, to be the Legislators and Governors of this Continent for the time being: whose peace and happiness, may GOD preserve. AMEN. . . .

But where, say some, is the King of America? I'll tell you, friend, he reigns above, and doth not make havoc of mankind like the Royal Brute of Great Britain. Yet that we may not appear to be defective even in earthly honours, let a day be solemnly set apart for proclaiming the Charter; let it be brought forth placed on the Divine Law, the Word of God; let a crown be placed thereon, by which the world may know, that so far as we approve of monarchy, that in America the law is king. For as in absolute governments the King is law, so in free countries the law ought to be king; and there ought to be no other. But lest any ill use should afterwards arise, let the Crown at the conclusion of the ceremony be demolished, and scattered among the people whose right it is.

2. The Declaration of Independence

In June of 1776, the Continental Congress appointed a committee of five members including Thomas Jefferson, Benjamin Franklin, John Adams, Roger Sherman and Robert R. Livingston, to prepare a formal declaration of independence; but not until July 2, 1776 was a formal resolution adopted to dissolve the connection between America and Great Britain. Two days later, the Continental Congress gave its approval to the Declaration of Independence which had been drafted to give the reasons for the action already taken. Thomas Jefferson wrote most of the draft of the Declaration with considerable help from Benjamin Franklin and John Adams. The following selection is the preamble that preceded the list of grievances enumerated in the rest of the Declaration of Independence. This preamble offers us a capsule summary of the philosophy of government which was shared by the people who supported the American Revolution. Read it carefully and consider the following questions:

1. What are the natural rights of men as defined in the Declaration of Independence?
2. What is the only just basis for the powers of government?
3. What are the proper goals of government as defined in the Declaration of Independence?

When in the Course of human events, it becomes necessary for one people to dissolve the political bands, which have connected them with another, and to assume among the powers of the earth, the separate and equal station to which the Laws of Nature and of Nature's God entitle them, a decent respect to the opinions of mankind requires that they should declare the causes which impel them to the separation. — We hold these truths to be self-evident, that all men are created equal, that they are endowed by their Creator with certain unalienable Rights, that among these are Life, Liberty and the pursuit of Happiness. — That to secure these rights, Governments are instituted among Men, deriving their just powers from the consent of the governed, — That whenever any Form of Government becomes destructive of these ends, it is the Right of the People to alter or to abolish it, and to institute new Government, laying its foundation on such principles and organizing its powers in such form, as to them shall seem most likely to effect their Safety and Happiness. Prudence, indeed, will dictate that Governments long established should not be changed for light and transient causes; and accordingly all experience hath shewn, that mankind are more disposed to suffer, while evils are sufferable, than to right themselves by abolishing the forms to which they are accustomed. But when a long train of abuses and usurpations, pursuing invariably the same Object evinces a design to reduce them under absolute Despotism, it is their right, it is their duty, to throw off such Government, and to provide new Guards for their future security.

3. The Virginia Declaration of Rights*

Virginia was one of the first of the states to draft a new constitution when it became clear that the tide of events was moving America towards independence. Indeed, the Virginia Constitution was drafted in the two months before independence was declared,

---

* From Francis N. Thorpe (ed.), *The Federal and State Constitutions* (House of Representatives Document No. 357, Government Printing Office, Washington, 1909), Vol. VII, pp. 3813–3814, Sections 1–16.

and adopted on June 29, 1776. Americans everywhere probably agreed with John Adams' statement that "we all look up to Virginia for examples." Thus, the Virginia Declaration of Rights was a notable statement of political and legal principles which was a model for other state constitutions of the period. Read the following provisions of the Virginia Declaration of Rights carefully and consider the following questions:

1. Does the Virginia Declaration of Rights contain the same ideas about the rights of man and the proper basis of government as the Declaration of Independence?
2. What specific political rights are guaranteed to the people? What legal rights are guaranteed to men accused of crimes? What rights of speech, thought, and belief are guaranteed?
3. Does the specific enumeration of rights in the Virginia Constitution help you understand what is meant by the rights of "Life, Liberty and the pursuit of Happiness" referred to in the Declaration of Independence?

A declaration of rights made by the representatives of the good people of Virginia, assembled in full and free convention; which rights do pertain to them and their posterity, as the basis and foundation of government.

SECTION 1. That all men are by nature equally free and independent, and have certain inherent rights, of which, when they enter into a state of society, they cannot, by any compact, deprive or divest their posterity; namely the enjoyment of life and liberty, with the means of acquiring and possessing property, and pursuing and obtaining happiness and safety.

SEC. 2. That all power is vested in, and consequently derived from, the people; that magistrates are their trustees and servants, and at all times amenable to them.

SEC. 3. That government is, or ought to be, instituted for the common benefit, protection, and security of the people, nation, or community; of all the various modes and forms of government, that is best which is capable of producing the greatest degree of happiness and safety, and is most effectually secured against the danger of maladministration; and that, when any government shall be found inadequate or contrary to these purposes, a majority of the community hath an indubitable, inalienable, and indefeasible right to reform, alter, or abolish it, in such manner as shall be judged most conducive to the public weal.

sec. 4. That no man, or set of men, are entitled to exclusive or separate emoluments or privileges from the community, but in consideration of public services; which, not being descendible, neither ought the offices of magistrate, legislator, or judge to be hereditary.

sec. 5. That the legislative and executive powers of the State should be separate and distinct from the judiciary; and that the members of the two first may be restrained from oppression, by feeling and participating the burdens of the people, they should, at fixed periods, be reduced to a private station, return into that body from which they were originally taken, and the vacancies be supplied by frequent, certain, and regular elections, in which all, or any part of the former members, to be again eligible, or ineligible, as the laws shall direct.

sec. 6. That elections of members to serve as representatives of the people, in assembly, ought to be free; and that all men, having sufficient evidence of permanent common interest with, and attachment to, the community, have the right of suffrage, and cannot be taxed or deprived of their property for public uses, without their own consent, or that of their representatives so elected, nor bound by any law to which they have not, in like manner, assembled, for the public good.

sec. 7. That all power of suspending laws, or the execution of laws, by any authority, without consent of the representatives of the people, is injurious to their rights, and ought not to be exercised.

sec. 8. That in all capital or criminal prosecutions a man hath a right to demand the cause and nature of his accusation, to be confronted with the accusers and witnesses, to call for evidence in his favor, and to a speedy trial by an impartial jury of twelve men of his vicinage, without whose unanimous consent he cannot be found guilty; nor can he be compelled to give evidence against himself; that no man be deprived of his liberty, except by the law of the land or the judgment of his peers.

SEC. 9. That excessive bail ought not to be required, nor excessive fines imposed, nor cruel and unusual punishments inflicted.

SEC. 10. That general warrants, whereby an officer or messenger may be commanded to search suspected places without evidence of a fact committed, or to seize any person or persons not named, or whose offence is not particularly described and supported by evidence, are grievous and oppressive, and ought not to be granted.

SEC. 11. That in controversies respecting property, and in suits between man and man, the ancient trial by jury is preferable to any other, and ought to be held sacred.

SEC. 12. That the freedom of the press is one of the great bulwarks of liberty, and can never be restrained but by despotic governments.

SEC. 13. That a well-regulated militia, composed of the body of the people, trained to arms, is the proper, natural, and safe defence of a free State; that standing armies, in time of peace, should be avoided, as dangerous to liberty; and that in all cases the military should be under strict subordination to, and governed by, the civil power.

SEC. 14. That the people have a right to uniform government; and, therefore, that no government separate from, or independent of the government of Virginia, ought to be erected or established within the limits thereof.

SEC. 15. That no free government, or the blessings of liberty, can be preserved to any people, but by a firm adherence to justice, moderation, temperance, frugality, and virtue, and by frequent recurrence to fundamental principles.

SEC. 16. That religion, or the duty which we owe to our Creator, and the manner of discharging it, can be directed only by reason and conviction, not by force or violence; and therefore all men are equally entitled to the free exercise of religion, according to the dictates of conscience; and that it is the mutual duty of all to practise Christian forbearance, love, and charity towards each other.

4. The Massachusetts Bill of Rights*

The Massachusetts Constitution of 1780 was unusual because of the procedure used in the framing and the adoption of the document. Virginia and other states had allowed their legislatures to assume the task of drafting a constitution and declaring it to be in force. In Massachusetts, it was decided that the people as a whole must endow the government with a constitution and not vice versa. Accordingly a special convention to draft a Constitution was chosen by the people of the towns, and the document prepared by the Convention was then submitted to the people in the towns for ratification. Hence the Massachusetts Constitution was a charter which came very close to being an expression of the consensus of the people. Read the provisions of the Massachusetts Bill of Rights carefully and consider these questions:

1. In what major ways is the Massachusetts Bill of Rights similar to the Virginia Declaration of Rights?
2. In what significant ways is the Massachusetts Bill of Rights different from the Virginia Declaration of Rights? How is religious worship to be regulated?
3. What kind of emphasis is placed on the relationship of executive, legislative and judicial powers in the organization of government?

Preamble

The end of the institution, maintenance, and administration of government, is to secure the existence of the body politic, to protect it, and to furnish the individuals who compose it with the

° From Francis N. Thorpe (ed.), *The Federal and State Constitutions* (House of Representatives Document No. 357, Government Printing Office, Washington, D.C., 1909). Vol. III, pp. 1888–1893, Preamble and Articles i–xxx.

power of enjoying in safety and tranquillity their natural rights, and the blessings of life: and whenever these great objects are not obtained, the people have a right to alter the government, and to take measures necessary for their safety, prosperity, and happiness.

The body politic is formed by a voluntary association of individuals: it is a social compact, by which the whole people covenants with each citizen, and each citizen with the whole people, that all shall be governed by certain laws for the common good. It is the duty of the people, therefore, in framing a constitution of government, to provide for an equitable mode of making laws, as well as for an impartial interpretation and a faithful execution of them; that every man may, at all times, find his security in them.

We, therefore, the people of Massachusetts, acknowledging, with grateful hearts, the goodness of the great Legislator of the universe, in affording us, in the course of His providence, an opportunity, deliberately and peaceably, without fraud, violence, or surprise, of entering into an original, explicit, and solemn compact with each other; and of forming a new constitution of civil government, for ourselves and posterity; and devoutly imploring His direction in so interesting a design, do agree upon, ordain, and establish, the following *Declaration of Rights, and Frame of Government,* as the CONSTITUTION OF THE COMMONWEALTH OF MASSACHUSETTS.

A Declaration of the Rights of the Inhabitants of the Commonwealth of Massachusetts

ARTICLE I. All men are born free and equal, and have certain natural, essential, and unalienable rights; among which may be reckoned the right of enjoying and defending their lives and liberties; that of acquiring, possessing, and protecting property; in fine, that of seeking and obtaining their safety and happiness.

II. It is the right as well as the duty of all men in society, publicly, and at stated seasons, to worship the SUPREME BEING, the great Creator and Preserver of the universe. And no subject shall be hurt, molested, or restrained, in his person, liberty, or estate, for worshipping God in the manner and season most agreeable to the dictates of his own conscience; or for his religious profession of sentiments; provided he doth not disturb the public peace, or obstruct others in their religious worship.

III. As the happiness of a people, and the good order and preservation of civil government, essentially depend upon piety, religion, and morality; and as these cannot be generally diffused through a community but by the institution of the public worship of God, and of public instructions in piety, religion, and morality: Therefore, to promote their happiness, and to secure the good order and preservation of their government, the people of this commonwealth have a right to invest their legislature with power to authorize and require, and the legislature shall, from time to time, authorize and require, the several towns, parishes, precincts, and other bodies politic, or religious societies, to make suitable provision, at their own expense, for the institution of the public worship of God, and for the support and maintenance of public Protestant teachers of piety, religion, and morality, in all cases where such provision shall not be made voluntarily.

And the people of this commonwealth have also a right to, and do, invest their legislature with authority to enjoin upon all the subjects an attendance upon the instructions of the public teachers aforesaid, at stated times and seasons, if there be any on whose instructions they can conscientiously and conveniently attend.

Provided, notwithstanding, that the several towns, parishes, precincts, and other bodies politic, or religious societies, shall, at all times, have the exclusive right of electing their public teachers, and of contracting with them for their support and maintenance.

And all moneys paid by the subject to the support of public worship, and of the public teachers aforesaid, shall, if he require it, be uniformly applied to the support of the public teacher or teachers of his own religious sect or denomination, provided there be any on whose instructions he attends; otherwise it may be paid towards the support of the teacher or teachers of the parish or precinct in which the said moneys are raised.

And every denomination of Christians, demeaning themselves peaceably, and as good subjects of the commonwealth, shall be equally under the protection of the law: and no subordination of any one sect or denomination to another shall ever be established by law.

IV. The people of this commonwealth have the sole and exclusive right of governing themselves, as a free, sovereign, and independent state; and do, and forever hereafter shall, exercise and enjoy every power, jurisdiction, and right, which is not, or may not hereafter be, by them expressly delegated to the United States of America, in Congress assembled.

V. All power residing originally in the people, and being derived from them, the several magistrates and officers of government, vested with authority, whether legislative, executive, or judicial, are their substitutes and agents, and are at all times accountable to them.

VI. No man, nor corporation, or association of men, have any other title to obtain advantages, or particular and exclusive privileges, distinct from those of the community, than what arises from the consideration of services rendered to the public; and this title being in nature neither hereditary, nor transmissible to children, or descendants, or relations by blood, the idea of a man born a magistrate, law-giver, or judge, is absurd and unnatural.

VII. Government is instituted for the common good; for the protection, safety, prosperity, and happiness of the people; and not for the profit, honor, or private interest of any one man, family, or class of men: Therefore the people alone have an incontestible unalienable, and indefeasible right to institute government; and to reform, alter, or totally change the same, when their protection, safety, prosperity, and happiness require it.

VIII. In order to prevent those who are vested with authority from becoming oppressors, the people have a right, at such periods and in such manner as they shall establish by their frame of government, to cause their public officers to return to private life; and to fill up vacant places by certain and regular elections and appointments.

IX. All elections ought to be free; and all the inhabitants of this commonwealth, having such qualifications as they shall establish by their frame of government, have an equal right to elect officers, and to be elected, for public employments.

X. Each individual of the society has a right to be protected by it in the enjoyment of his life, liberty, and property, according to standing laws. He is obliged, consequently, to contribute his share to the expense of this protection; to give his personal service, or an equivalent, when necessary; but no part of the property of any individual can, with justice, be taken from him, or applied to public uses, without his own consent, or that of the representative body of the people. In fine, the people of this commonwealth are not controllable by any other laws than those to which their constitutional representative body have given their consent. And whenever the public exigencies require that the property of any individual should be appropriated to public uses, he shall receive a reasonable compensation therefor.

XI. Every subject of the commonwealth ought to find a certain remedy, by having recourse to the laws, for all injuries or wrongs which he may receive in his person, property, or character. He ought to obtain right and justice freely, and without being obliged to purchase it; completely, and without any denial; promptly, and without delay, conformably to the laws.

XII. No subject shall be held to answer for any crimes or offence, until the same is fully and plainly, substantially, and formally, described to him; or be compelled to accuse, or furnish evidence against himself. And every subject shall have a right to produce all proofs that may be favorable to him; to meet the witnesses against him face to face, and to be fully heard in his defence by himself, or his counsel, at his election. And no subject shall be arrested, imprisoned, despoiled, or deprived of his property, immunities, or privileges, put out of the protection of the law, exiled, or deprived of his life, liberty, or estate, but by the judgment of his peers, or the law of the land.

And the legislature shall not make any law that shall subject any person to a capital or infamous punishment, excepting for the government of the army and navy, without trial by jury.

XIII. In criminal prosecutions, the verification of facts, in the vicinity where they happen, is one of the greatest securities of the life, liberty, and property of the citizen.

XIV. Every subject has a right to be secure from all unreasonable search, and seizures, of his person, his houses, his papers, and all his possessions. All warrants, therefore, are contrary to this right, if the cause or foundation of them be not previously supported by oath or affirmation, and if the order in the warrant to a civil officer, to make search in suspected places, or to arrest one or more suspected persons, or to seize their property, be not accompanied with a special designation of the persons or objects of search, arrest, or seizure; and no warrant ought to be issued but in cases, and with the formalities prescribed by the laws.

XV. In all controversies concerning property, and in all suits between two or more persons, except in cases in which it has heretofore been otherways used and practised, the parties have a right to a trial by jury; and this method of procedure shall be held sacred, unless, in causes arising on the high seas, and such as relate to mariners' wages, the legislature shall hereafter find it necessary to alter it.

XVI. The liberty of the press is essential to the security of freedom in a state it ought not, therefore, to be restricted in this commonwealth.

XVII. The people have a right to keep and to bear arms for the common defence. And as, in time of peace, armies are dangerous to liberty, they ought not to be maintained without the consent of the legislature; and the military power shall always be held in an exact subordination to the civil authority, and be governed by it.

XVIII. A frequent recurrence to the fundamental principles of the constitution, and a constant adherence to those of piety, justice, moderation, temperance, industry, and frugality, are absolutely necessary to preserve the advantages of liberty, and to maintain a free government. The people ought, consequently, to have a particular attention to all those principles, in the choice of their officers and representatives: and they have a right to require of their lawgivers and magistrates an exact and constant observance of them, in the formation and execution of the laws necessary for the good administration of the commonwealth.

XIX. The people have a right, in an orderly and peaceable manner, to assemble to consult upon the common good; give instructions to their representatives, and to request of the legislative body, by the way of addresses, petitions, or remonstrances, redress of the wrongs done them, and of the grievances they suffer.

XX. The power of suspending the laws, or the execution of the laws, ought never to be exercised but by the legislature, or by authority derived from it, to be exercised in such particular cases only as the legislature shall expressly provide for.

XXI. The freedom of deliberation, speech, and debate, in either house of the legislature, is so essential to the rights of the people, that it cannot be the foundation of any accusation or prosecution, action or complaint, in any other court or place whatsoever.

XXII. The legislature ought frequently to assemble for the redress of grievances, for correcting, strengthening, and confirming the laws, and for making new laws, as the common good may require.

XXIII. No subsidy, charge, tax, impost, or duties ought to be established, fixed, laid, or levied, under any pretext whatsoever, without the consent of the people or their representatives in the legislature.

XXIV. Laws made to punish for actions done before the existence of such laws, and which have not been declared crimes by preceding laws, are unjust, oppressive, and inconsistent with the fundamental principles of a free government.

XXV. No subject ought, in any case, or in any time, to be declared guilty of treason or felony by the legislature.

XXVI. No magistrate or court of law shall demand excessive bail or sureties, impose excessive fines, or inflict cruel or unusual punishments.

XXVII. In time of peace, no soldier ought to be quartered in any house without the consent of the owner; and in time of war, such quarters ought not to be made but by the civil magistrate, in a manner ordained by the legislature.

XXVIII. No person can in any case be subject to law-martial, or to any penalties or pains, by virtue of that law, except those employed in the army or navy, and except the militia in actual service, but by authority of the legislature.

XXIX. It is essential to the preservation of the rights of every individual, his life, liberty, property, and character, that there be an impartial interpretation of the laws, and administration of justice. It is the right of every citizen to be tried by judges as free, impartial, and independent as the lot of humanity will admit. It is, therefore, not only the best policy, but for the security of the rights of the people, and of every citizen, that the judges of the supreme judicial court should hold their offices as long as they behave themselves well; and that they should have honorable salaries ascertained and established by standing laws.

XXX. In the government of this commonwealth, the legislative department shall never exercise the executive and judicial powers, or either of them: the executive shall never exercise the legislative and judicial powers, or either of them: the judicial shall never exercise the legislative and executive powers, or either of them: to the end it may be a government of laws and not of men.

OUR second step in the analysis of conflict and consensus in the American Revolution will be an investigation of some documents that refer to matters of controversy and conflict. The statements which are included in this part of our volume cannot include all that we need to know about the conflicts of the Revolutionary period, but they can give us valuable clues concerning the types of conflict which took place. The selections which reveal points of conflict are arranged in three groups: those that deal with the structure of government; those that deal with questions of status — whether "the rich, well-born and able" should continue to enjoy special privileges and power; and those that deal with the freedom of religion. By studying these documents we may be able to get a clearer idea of whether these conflicts were serving to disrupt or to readjust the consensus of the Revolutionary generation.

Part 3

Points of Conflict

A. *The Organization of Government*

5. "The People the Best Governors" *

Although there was considerable agreement among Americans of the Revolutionary generation about the natural rights of man and the proper ends of government, there was disagreement about the specific ways to construct a government and to distribute power among the various branches of government. There were many who wished to make government as responsive as possible to the will of the majority of the people. There were others who feared power; who believed that any kind of concentrated power was dangerous — whether it was the power of the majority, or the power of the executive, or the legislature. The following selection is from an anonymous pamphlet entitled "The People The Best Governors" and published in New Hampshire in 1776. In this pamphlet, the author calls for a popular form of government. Read the selection carefully and try to answer these questions:

1. Why, in the opinion of the author, are the common people the best guardians of their own liberties?
2. What power should be separated from the legislature?
3. Why is the author of this pamphlet opposed to an upper house in the assembly elected by the people?

The just power of a free people respects first the making and secondly the executing of laws. The liberties of a people are

* From Frederick Chase, *A History of Dartmouth College and the Town of Hanover* (Cambridge, Mass., 1891), Vol. I, pp. 655–657, abridged.

chiefly, I may say entirely guarded by having the controul of these two branches in their own hands . . .

Were the people of the different counties numerous and wealthy enough, with that degree of knowledge which is common in many parts of the continent, every freeman might then have a hand in making laws to govern himself by, as well as in appointing the person to execute them; but the people of these States are very unequally and thinly settled, which puts us upon seeking some mode of governing by a representative body. The freemen give up in this way just so much of their natural right as they find absolutely convenient, on account of the disadvantages in their personal acting. The question now arises, how far they can with safety deposit this power of theirs into other hands? To this I answer that where there are representatives who hold the legislature, their power ought never to extend any further than barely the making of laws. For what matters it, whether they themselves execute the laws, or appoint persons to do it in their stead, since these very persons, being only creatures of their own appointment, will be induced by interest to act agreeable to their will and pleasure. Indeed upon this plan the greatest corruption may take place, — for should there be in some important affairs very unjust decisions, where could the injury gain redress? Iniquity might be supported by the executioners of it; they out of the reach of the people, from whom they do not derive their authority; and the legislative body, as they are not the immediate perpetrators, may be often skreened from just reproach.

Perhaps it will be said by some that the people are sufficiently guarded against infringements of this nature, as their representatives are chosen only for a certain time, may be called to an account for any misconduct in their business, and withal are liable to be turned out by their constituents at any time. There is indeed something plausible in all this; but it will vanish when we consider that these representatives, while they act as such, being supreme in legislation and in the appointing and supporting the executors of law, may by these advantages assume to themselves a lasting, unlimited power. And I beg of any one to tell me what will prevent it, if they have only art, and are generally agreed among themselves.

But it seems there is another objection started by some: That the common people are not under so good advantages to choose judges, sheriffs, and other executive officers as their representatives are. This is a mere delusion, which many have taken in, and, if I may be allowed a vulgar expression, the objectors in this instance put the cart before the horse. For they say that the people have wisdom and knowledge enough to appoint proper persons through a State to make laws, but not to execute them. It is much easier to execute, than to make and regulate the system of laws, and upon this single consideration the force of the objection fails: The more simple, and the more immediately dependent . . . the authority is upon the people the better, because it must be granted that they themselves are the best guardians of their own liberties.

2dly Upon the above principles we will proceed farther, and say that if there be a distinct negative power over those that enact the laws, it can by no means derive it from them as representatives of the people, and for these reasons: As far as there is any power over the rights of the people, so far they themselves are divested of it. Now, by chusing representatives to make laws for them, they put that power out of their own hands; yet they do not deposit it into the hands of their representatives to give to others, but to exercise it in their room and stead. — Therefore, I say, for the representatives to appoint a council with a negative authority, is to give away that power, which they have no right to do, because they themselves derived it from the people.

But it will be enquired whether the inhabitants themselves, through a State, cannot consistently make a negating body over those that form the laws? To this I answer that there is no real absurdity in their taking such a step: But upon this plan those that are called representatives have only a partial right as such; for they have a delegated power from the people to act no farther than this negative body concurs. Now this said negative body are likewise virtually the representatives of the people, and derive just so much authority from them as will make up the defect of the others, viz., that of confirming. They have been generally named a council in our American States, though they have really acted in a legislative capacity, and seem rather to answer the idea of a *senate,* which was hereditary at Rome, but here elective . . .

To conclude, I do not say that it is expedient to choose a Senate, if I may so call it, with such a negative power as before mentioned; but rather propose, whether a council of advice would not answer better purposes, and that inequality be thereby prevented, which is sometimes occasioned by two distinct fountains of power.

6. JOHN ADAMS: "Thoughts on Government" *

John Adams was horrified by such ideas as were expressed in The People The Best Governors. *He was even more dismayed when the revolutionary leaders of Pennsylvania adopted a constitution in 1776 which concentrated all power in a single popularly elected assembly without any checks or balances. John Adams was a firm believer in the separation of powers and the limitation of all governing power by means of carefully constructed checks and balances. The Massachusetts Constitution of 1780 is largely the product of his thinking about the proper organization of government. The following selection is taken from an essay entitled "Thoughts on Government" which John Adams wrote to advise political leaders in other states about the construction of a well-ordered government. Read this selection carefully and consider the following questions:*

1. What, according to Adams, is wrong with assigning all powers to a single popular assembly?

* From Charles F. Adams (ed.), *The Works of John Adams* (Boston, 1865), Vol. IV, pp. 194–197, 198–199, abridged.

2. How does Adams propose to develop checks upon the popular assembly?
3. Why does he believe that an independent judiciary is necessary?

As good government is an empire of laws, how shall your laws be made? In a large society, inhabiting an extensive country, it is impossible that the whole should assemble to make laws. The first necessary step, then, is to depute power from the many to a few of the most wise and good. But by what rules shall you choose your representatives? Agree upon the number and qualifications of persons who shall have the benefit of choosing, or annex this privilege to the inhabitants of a certain extent of ground.

The principal difficulty lies, and the greatest care should be employed, in constituting this representative assembly. It should be in miniature an exact portrait of the people at large. It should think, feel, reason, and act like them. That it may be the interest of this assembly to do strict justice at all times, it should be an equal representation, or, in other words, equal interests among the people should have equal interests in it. Great care should be taken to effect this, and to prevent unfair, partial, and corrupt elections. Such regulations, however, may be better made in times of greater tranquillity than the present; and they will spring up themselves naturally, when all the powers of government come to be in the hands of the people's friends. At present, it will be safest to proceed in all established modes, to which the people have been familiarized by habit.

A representation of the people in one assembly being obtained, a question arises, whether all the powers of government, legislative, executive, and judicial, shall be left in this body? I think a people cannot be long free, nor ever happy, whose government is in one assembly. My reasons for this opinion are as follows: —

1. A single assembly is liable to all the vices, follies, and frailties of an individual; subject to fits of humor, starts of passion, flights of enthusiasm, partialities, or prejudice, and conse-

quently productive of hasty results and absurd judgements. And all the errors ought to be corrected and defects supplied by some controlling power.

2. A single assembly is apt to be avaricious, and in time will not scruple to exempt itself from burdens, which it will lay, without compunction, on its constituents.

3. A single assembly is apt to grow ambitious, and after a time will not hesitate to vote itself perpetual. This was one fault of the Long Parliament; but more remarkably of Holland, whose assembly first voted themselves from annual to septennial, then for life, and after a course of years, that all vacancies happening by death or otherwise, should be filled by themselves, without any application to constituents at all.

4. A representative assembly, although extremely well qualified, and absolutely necessary, as a branch of the legislative, is unfit to exercise the executive power, for want of two essential properties, secrecy and despatch.

5. A representative assembly is still less qualified for the judicial power, because it is too numerous, too slow, and too little skilled in the laws.

6. Because a single assembly, possessed of all the powers of government, would make arbitrary laws for their own interest, execute all laws arbitrarily for their own interest, and adjudge all controversies in their own favor.

But shall the whole power of legislation rest in one assembly? Most of the foregoing reasons apply equally to prove that the legislative power ought to be more complex; to which we may add, that if the legislative power is wholly in one assembly, and the executive in another, or in a single person, these two powers will oppose and encroach upon each other, until the contest shall end in war, and the whole power, legislative and executive, be usurped by the strongest.

The judicial power, in such case, could not mediate, or hold the balance between the two contending powers, because the legislative would undermine it. And this shows the necessity, too, of giving the executive power a negative upon the legislative, otherwise this will be continually encroaching upon that.

To avoid these dangers, let a distinct assembly be constituted, as a mediator between the two extreme branches of the legislature, that which represents the people, and that which is vested with the executive power.

Let the representative assembly then elect by ballot, from among themselves or their constituents, or both, a distinct assembly, which, for the sake of perspicuity, we will call a council. It may consist of any number you please, say twenty or thirty, and should have a free and independent exercise of its judgment, and consequently a negative voice in the legislature.

These two bodies, thus constituted, and made integral parts of the legislature, let them unite, and by joint ballot choose a governor, who, after being stripped of most of those badges of domination, called prerogatives, should have a free and independent exercise of his judgment, and be made also an integral part of the legislature. This, I know, is liable to objections; and, if you please, you may make him only president of the council, as in Connecticut. But as the governor is to be invested with the executive power, with consent of council, I think he ought to have a negative upon the legislative. If he is annually elective, as he ought to be, he will always have so much reverence and affection for the people, their representatives and counsellors, that, although you give him an independent exercise of his judgment, he will seldom use it in opposition to the two houses, except in cases the public utility of which would be conspicuous; and some such cases would happen.

The dignity and stability of government in all its branches, the morals of the people, and every blessing of society depend so much upon an upright and skillful administration of justice, that the judicial power ought to be distinct from both the legislative and executive, and independent upon both, that so it may be a check upon both, as both should be checks upon that. The judges, therefore, should be always men of learning and experience in the laws, of exemplary morals, great patience, calmness, coolness, and attention. Their minds should not be distracted with jarring interests; they should not be dependent upon any man, or body of men. To these ends, they should hold estates for life in their offices; or, in other words, their commissions should be during good behavior, and their salaries ascertained and established by law. For misbehavior, the grand inquest of the colony, the house of representatives, should impeach them before the governor and council, where they should have time and opportunity to make their defence; but, if convicted, should be removed from their offices, and subjected to such other punishment as shall be thought proper.

7. The Articles of Confederation

The attempt to draft a charter of government for the union of thirteen states during the Revolution was a matter of prolonged controversy. The Articles of Confederation emerged from extended debates in the Continental Congress in 1776 and 1777 and were not finally ratified until 1781. Even when the Articles of Confederation were ratified, there was widespread criticism of the organization of government which it created. The following articles in the Articles of Confederation raised the most fundamental points of controversy. Read them carefully and consider the following questions:

1. Where was sovereign power located by the Articles of Confederation?
2. How was revenue to be raised in the new government?
3. What powers were given to the Congress of the Confederation? How were these powers limited?

THE ARTICLES OF CONFEDERATION AND PERPETUAL UNION

ART. 2. Each State retains its sovereignty, freedom and independence, and every power, jurisdiction, and right, which is not by this confederation expressly delegated to the United States, in Congress assembled.

ART. 8. All charges of war and all other expences, that shall be incurred for the common defence or general welfare, and allowed by the United States, in Congress assembled, shall be defrayed out of a common treasury, which shall be supplied by the several states, in proportion to the value of all land within each State, granted to or surveyed for any person, as such land and the buildings and improvements thereon shall be estimated according to such mode as the United States, in Congress assembled, shall, from time to time, direct and appoint.

The taxes for paying that proportion shall be laid and levied by the authority and direction of the legislatures of the several states, within the time agreed upon by the United States, in Congress assembled.

ART. 9. The United States, in Congress assembled, shall have the sole and exclusive right and power of determining on peace and war, except in the cases mentioned in the 6th article; of sending and receiving ambassadors; entering into treaties and alliances, provided that no treaty of commerce shall be made, whereby the legislative power of the respective states shall be restrained from imposing such imposts and duties on foreigners as their own people are subjected to, or from prohibiting the exportation or importation of any species of goods or commodities whatsoever; of establishing rules for deciding, in all cases, what captures on land or water shall be legal, and in what manner prizes, taken by land or naval forces in the service of the United States, shall be divided or appropriated; of granting letters of marque and reprisal in times of peace; appointing courts for the trial of piracies and felonies committed on the high seas, and establishing courts for receiving and determining, finally, appeals in all cases of captures; provided, that no member of Congress shall be appointed a judge of any of the said courts . . .

The United States, in Congress assembled, shall also have the sole and exclusive right and power of regulating the alloy and value of coin struck by their own authority, or by that of the respective states; fixing the standard of weights and measures throughout the United States; regulating the trade and managing all affairs with the Indians not members of any of the states; provided that the legislative right of any State within its own limits be not infringed or violated; establishing and regulating post offices from one State to another throughout all the United States, and exacting such postage on the papers passing through the same as may be requisite to defray the expences of the said office; appointing all officers of the land forces in the service of the United States, excepting regimental officers; appointing all the officers of the naval forces, and commissioning all officers whatever in the service of the United States; making rules for the government and regulation of the said land and naval forces, and directing their operations.

The United States, in Congress assembled, shall have authority to appoint a committee to sit in the recess of Congress, to be denominated "a Committee of the States," and to consist of one delegate from each State, and to appoint such other committees and civil officers as may be necessary for managing the general affairs of the United States, under their direction; to appoint one of their number to preside; provided that no person be allowed to serve in the office of president more than one year in any term of three years; to ascertain the necessary sums of money to be raised for the service of the United States, and to appropriate and apply the same for defraying the public expences; to borrow money or emit bills on the credit of the United States, transmitting, every half year, to the respective states, an account of the sums of money so borrowed or emitted; to build and equip a navy; to agree upon the number of land forces, and to make requisitions from each State for its quota, in proportion to the number of white inhabitants in such State; which requisitions shall be binding; and, thereupon, the legislature of each State shall appoint the regimental officers, raise the men, and cloathe, arm, and equip them in a soldier-like manner, at the expence of the United States; and the officers and men so cloathed, armed, and equipped, shall march to the place appointed and within the time agreed on by the United States, in Congress assembled; but if the United States, in Congress assembled, shall, on consideration of circumstances, judge proper that any States should not raise men, or should raise a smaller number than its quota, and that any other State should raise a greater number of men than the quota thereof, such extra number shall be raised, officered, cloathed, armed, and equipped in the same manner as the quota of such State, unless the legislature of such State shall judge that such extra number cannot be safely spared out of the same, in which case they shall raise, officer, cloathe, arm, and equip as many of such extra number as they judge can be safely spared. And the officers and men so cloathed, armed, and equipped, shall march to the place appointed and within the time agreed on by the United States, in Congress assembled.

The United States, in Congress assembled, shall never engage in a war, nor grant letters of marque and reprisal in time of peace, nor enter into any treaties or alliances, nor coin money, nor regulate the value thereof, nor ascertain the sums and expences necessary for the defence and welfare of the United States, or any of them: nor emit bills, nor borrow money on the credit of the United States, nor appropriate money, nor agree upon the number of vessels of war to be built or purchased, or the number of land or sea forces to be raised, nor appoint a commander in chief of the army or navy, unless nine states assent to the same; nor shall a question on any other point, except for adjourning from day to day, be determined, unless by the votes of a majority of the United States, in Congress assembled.

The Congress of the United States shall have power to adjourn to any time within the year, and to any place within the United States, so that no period of adjournment be for a longer duration than the space of six months, and shall publish the journal of their proceedings monthly, except such parts thereof, relating to treaties, alliances or military operations, as, in their judgment, require secrecy; and the yeas and nays of the delegates of each State on any question shall be entered on the journal, when it is desired by any delegate; and the delegates of a State, or any of them, at his, or their request, shall be furnished with a transcript of the said journal, except such parts as are above expected, to lay before the legislatures of the several states.

8. ALEXANDER HAMILTON: "The Confederation . . . is neither fit for war nor peace." *

Alexander Hamilton was a young man of great ability and influence during the Revolutionary years. He served on General Washington's military staff and was married to the daughter of one of the leading families in New York. He was highly critical of the Articles of Confederation and expressed objections of the most fundamental sort in letters to influential leaders. The following selection comes from a letter that Hamilton wrote in 1780 to James Duane, one of New York's delegates to the Continental Congress. Read this selection carefully and consider the following questions:

1. What does Hamilton think about the location of sovereign power in the Articles of Confederation?
2. What does Hamilton say about the "power of the purse"?
3. What is the problem of executive power as he sees it?

LIBERTY POLE, September 3, 1780.

DEAR SIR:

Agreeably to your request, and my promise, I sit down to give you my ideas of the defects of our present system, and the

* From John C. Hamilton (ed.), *The Works of Alexander Hamilton* (New York, 1850), Vol. I, pp. 150–154, abridged.

changes necessary to save us from ruin. They may, perhaps, be the reveries of a projector, rather than the sober views of a politician. You will judge of them, and make what use you please of them.

The fundamental defect is a want of power in Congress. It is hardly worth while to show in what this consists, as it seems to be universally acknowledged; or to point out how it has happened, as the only question is how to remedy it. It may, however, be said, that it has originated from three causes: an excess of the spirit of liberty, which has made the particular States show a jealousy of all power not in their own hands; and this jealousy has led them to exercise a right of judging in the last resort of the measures recommended by Congress, and of acting according to their own opinions of their propriety, or necessity; a diffidence, in Congress, of their own powers, by which they have been timid and indecisive in their resolutions: constantly making concessions to the States, till they have scarcely left themselves the shadow of power; a want of sufficient means at their disposal to answer the public exigencies, and of vigor to draw forth those means; which have occasioned them to depend on the States individually, to fulfill their engagements with the army; the consequence of which, has been to ruin their influence and credit with the army, to establish its dependence on each State separately, rather than *on them,* that is, rather than on the whole collectively.

It may be pleaded, that Congress had never any definite powers granted them, and, of course, could exercise none, could do nothing more than recommend. The manner in which Congress was appointed, would warrant, and the public good required, that they should have considered themselves as vested with full power *to preserve the republic from harm.* They have done many of the highest acts of sovereignty, which were always cheerfully submitted to: The declaration of independence; the declaration of war: the levying of an army; creating a navy; emitting money; making alliances with foreign powers; appointing a dictator, etc., etc. All these implications of a complete sovereignty were never

disputed, and ought to have been a standard for the whole conduct of administration. Undefined powers are discretionary powers, limited only by the object for which they were given; in the
present case, the independence and freedom of America. The
Confederation made no difference; for as it has not been generally
adopted, it had no operation. But from what I recollect of it,
Congress have even descended from the authority which the
spirit of that act gives them; while the particular States have no
further attended to it, than as it suited their pretensions and convenience. It would take too much time to enter into particular
instances, each of which separately might appear inconsiderable;
but united, are of serious import. I only mean to remark, not to
censure.

But the Confederation itself is defective, and requires to be
altered. It is neither fit for war nor peace. The idea of an uncon-
trollable sovereignty, in each State, over its internal police, will
defeat the other powers given to Congress, and make our union
feeble and precarious. There are instances without number,
where Acts, necessary for the general good, and which rise out of
the powers given to Congress, must interfere with the internal
police of the States; and there are as many instances in which
the particular States, by arrangements of internal police, can effectually, though indirectly, counteract the arrangements of Congress. You have already had examples of this, for which I refer
you to your own memory.

The Confederation gives the States, individually, too much influence in the affairs of the army. They should have nothing to
do with it. The entire formation and disposal of our military
forces, ought to belong to Congress. It is an essential cement of
the union: and it ought to be the policy of Congress, to destroy
all ideas of State attachments in the army, and make it look up
wholly to them. For this purpose, all appointments, promotions,
and provisions, whatsoever, ought to be made by them. It may be
apprehended that this may be dangerous to liberty. But nothing
appears more evident to me, than that we run much greater risk

of having a weak and disunited federal government, than one which will be able to usurp upon the rights of the people.

Already some of the lines of the army would obey their States in opposition to Congress, notwithstanding the pains we have taken to preserve the unity of the army. If any thing would hinder this, it would be the personal influence of the General; a melancholy and mortifying consideration.

The forms of our State constitutions, must always give them great weight in our affairs, and will make it too difficult to bend them to the pursuit of a common interest; too easy to oppose whatever they do not like: and to form partial combinations subversive of the general one. There is a wide difference between our situation, and that of an empire under one simple form of government, distributed into counties, provinces, or districts, which have no legislatures, but merely magistratical bodies, to execute the laws of a common sovereign. Here the danger is, that the sovereign will have too much power, and oppress the parts of which it is composed. In our case, that of an empire composed of confederated States; each with a government completely organized within itself, having all the means to draw its subjects to a close dependence on itself; the danger is directly the reverse. It is, that the common sovereign will not have power sufficient to unite the different members together, and direct the common forces to the interest and happiness of the whole . . .

The Confederation, too, gives the power of the purse too entirely to the State Legislatures. It should provide perpetual funds, in the disposal of Congress, by a land tax, poll tax, or the like. All imposts upon commerce ought to be laid by Congress, and appropriated to their use. For, without certain revenues, a Government can have no power. That power which holds the purse-strings absolutely, must rule. This seems to be a medium which, without making Congress altogether independent, will tend to give reality to its authority.

Another defect in our system, is want of method and energy in the administration. This has partly resulted from the other defect; but in a great degree from prejudice, and the want of a proper executive. Congress have kept the power too much in their own hands, and have meddled too much with details of every sort. Congress is, properly, a deliberative corps; and it forgets itself when it attempts to play the executive. It is impossible such a body, numerous as it is, constantly fluctuating, can ever act with sufficient decision, or with system. Two-thirds of the members, one half the time, cannot know what has gone before them, or what connection the subject in hand has to what has been transacted on former occasions. The members who have been more permanent, will only give information that promotes the side they espouse in the present case; and will as often mislead as enlighten. The variety of business must distract; and the proneness of every assembly to debate, must at all times delay.

B. *Status*

9. JOHN ADAMS: "Surely we must guard against this spirit" *

John Adams was no friend of the hereditary distinctions and titles of Great Britain. He wrote to a friend in 1776, "The dons . . . the grandees, the patricians . . . the nabobs, call them by what name you please, sigh, and groan . . . and foam, and curse, but all in vain . . . a more equal liberty than has prevailed in other parts of the earth, must be established in America." Nevertheless, Adams believed that wealth and birth were always closely linked to superior merit and talent among men. The following

* From Charles F. Adams (ed.), *The Works of John Adams* (Boston, 1865), Vol. II, pp. 420–421.

entry in John Adams' diary in 1775 reveals this sense of superior status as well as an attitude of irritation at the growing assertiveness of the common people. Read this selection carefully and consider the following question:

1. What is the basic fear which was troubling Adams when he wrote this account in his diary?

An event of the most trifling nature in appearance, and fit only to excite laughter in other times, struck me into a profound reverie, if not a fit of melancholy. I met a man who had sometimes been my client, and sometimes I had been against him. He, though a common horse-jockey, was sometimes in the right, and I had commonly been successful in his favor in our courts of law. He was always in the law, and had been sued in many actions at almost every court. As soon as he saw me, he came up to me, and his first salutation to me was, "Oh! Mr. Adams, what great things have you and your colleagues done for us! We can never be grateful enough to you. There are no courts of justice now in this Province, and I hope there never will be another." Is this the object for which I have been contending? said I to myself, for I rode along without any answer to this wretch. Are these the sentiments of such people, and how many of them are there in the country? Half the nation, for what I know; for half the nation are debtors, if not more, and these have been, in all countries, the sentiments of debtors. If the power of the country should get into such hands, and there is great danger that it will, to what purpose have we sacrificed our time, health, and everything else? Surely we must guard against this spirit, and these principles, or we shall repent of all our conduct. However, the good sense and integrity of the majority of the great body of the people came into my thoughts, for my relief, and the last resource was after all in a good Providence.

10. JOHN TRUMBULL: ". . . the rule of topsy-turvies" *

John Trumbull was a leading lawyer in Hartford, Connecticut, closely related to Governor Jonathan Trumbull. He had been a tutor at Yale for a time and developed a taste for literature that led him to try his hand at poetry. Trumbull's best efforts were his satirical poems, and the mock epic poem, M'Fingal, first printed in 1775, was his only popular and widely read work. Trumbull was a well-bred patriot; he did not like Tories, yet he also disapproved of the Sons of Liberty and their demagogic ways. The following verses are taken from a speech made by M'Fingal, the Tory squire, but the cutting edge of the satire is aimed primarily at the Sons of Liberty. Read the selection carefully and consider the following question:

1. How do these verses reveal prejudices based on ideas of class and status?

"Ye dupes to every factious rogue
And tavern-prating demagogue,
Whose tongue but rings, with sound more full,
On th' empty drumhead of his scull;
Behold you not what noisy fools
Use you, worse simpletons, for tools?
For Liberty, in your own by-sense,
Is but for crimes a patent license,
To break of law th' Egyptian yoke,
And throw the world in common stock;
Reduce all grievances and ills
To Magna Charta of your wills;
Establish cheats and frauds and nonsense,

* From John Trumbull, *M'Fingal, a Modern Epic Poem* (Hartford, 1856), pp. 99, 101–103, abridged.

Framed to the model of your conscience; . . .
And when by clamors and confusions,
Your freedom's grown a public nuisance,
Cry 'Liberty,' with powerful yearning,
As he does 'Fire!' whose house is burning;
Though he already has much more
Than he can find occasion for.
While every clown that tills the plains,
Though bankrupt in estate and brains,
By this new light transform'd to traitor,
Forsakes his plough to turn dictator,
Starts an haranguing chief of Whigs,
And drags you by the ears, like pigs.
All bluster, arm'd with factious license,
New-born at once to politicians.
Each leather-apron'd dunce, grown wise,
Presents his forward face t' advise,
And tatter'd legislators meet,
From every workshop through the street.
His goose the tailor finds no use in,
To patch and turn the Constitution;
The blacksmith comes with sledge and grate
To iron-bind the wheels of state;
The quack forbears his patients' souse,
To purge the Council and the House;
The tinker quits his moulds and doxies,
To cast assembly-men and proxies.
From dunghills deep of blackest hue,
You dirt-bred patriots spring to view,
To wealth and power and honors rise,
Like new-wing'd maggots changed to flies,
And fluttering round in high parade,
Strut in the robe, or gay cockade.
For in this ferment of the stream
The dregs have work'd up to the brim,

And by the rule of topsy-turvies,
The scum stands foaming on the surface.
You've caused your pyramid t' ascend,
And set it on the little end.
You've push'd and turn'd the whole world up-
Side down, and got yourselves at top,
While all the great ones of your state
Are crush'd beneath the popular weight . . ."

11. THOMAS PAINE: "Reflection on Titles" *

Unlike John Adams or John Trumbull, Tom Paine had no linger-
ing desire to uphold the superior social status of gentlemen of
wealth and learning. The following essay was written for the
Pennsylvania Magazine *in 1775. Read the essay carefully and*
answer the following question:

1. What does Paine think is the only true form of honor which should exist
   in a free society?

When I reflect on the pompous titles bestowed on unworthy
men, I feel an indignity that instructs me to despise the absurdity.
The *Honourable* plunder of his country, or the *Right Honourable*
murderer of mankind, create such a contrast of ideas as exhibit a
monster rather than a man. Virtue is inflamed at the violation,
and sober reason calls it nonsense.

Dignities and high sounding names have different effects on
different beholders. The lustre of the *Star* and the title of *My
Lord*, over-awe the superstitious vulgar, and forbid them to in-
quire into the character of the possessor: Nay more, they are, as
it were, bewitched to admire in the great, the vice they would

honestly condemn in themselves. This sacrifice of common sense is the certain badge which distinguishes slavery from freedom; for when men yield up the privilege of thinking, the last shadow of liberty quits the horizon.

But the reasonable freeman sees through the magic of a title, and examines the man before he approves him. To him the honours of the worthless serve to write their masters' vices in capitals, and their stars shine to no other end than to read them by. The possessors of undue honours are themselves sensible of this; for when their repeated guilt renders their persons unsafe, they disown their rank, and, like glow-worms, extinguish themselves into common reptiles, to avoid discovery. Thus Jeffries sunk into a fisherman, and his master escaped in the habit of a peasant.*

Modesty forbids men, separately or collectively, to assume titles. But as all honours, even that of Kings, originated from the public, the public may justly be called the fountain of true honour. And it is with much pleasure I have heard the title of *Honourable* applied to a body of men, who nobly disregarding private ease and interest for public welfare, have justly merited the address of The Honourable Continental Congress.

C. *Religious Freedom*

12. An Appeal of the Baptists to the General Court of Massachusetts†

In Massachusetts, New Hampshire and Connecticut, the Congregational Church had been the established church throughout the

* Paine is referring to the flight of King James II and his Lord Chancellor, George Jeffreys, from England during the Glorious Revolution of 1688.
† From Alvah Hovey, *Memoir of the Life and Times of the Rev. Isaac Backus* (Boston, 1859), pp. 241–242.

colonial period. *All inhabitants were compelled to pay taxes for the support of the Congregational Church and to attend its services. Gradually, in the years before the Revolution, a few religious groups were able to get exemption from these requirements. But exemption was only possible if you could prove that you were a member of some organized religious group which had a regularly conducted system of worship. Dissenting groups like the Baptists and Quakers protested against these infringements on their liberty to worship and their freedom of conscience. They were dismayed when the Massachusetts Constitution of 1780 continued many of the older requirements for the support of religion. The following protest by leading Baptists was sent to the General Court of Massachusetts in 1780 objecting to the religious articles in the new Constitution. Read this protest carefully and consider the following questions:*

1. For what reasons do the Baptists object to the power given to majority in each town to choose ministers and the forms of public worship?
2. Do you think that the Baptists' conception of religious liberty is closer to the ideas in the Declaration of Independence than Article III of the Massachusetts Bill of Rights?

"To the General Court of the Massachusetts, assembled at Boston, October, 1780.

"We, whose names are hereunto subscribed, inhabitants of this state, who are twenty-one years of age and above, of various religious denominations, enter our PROTEST against the power claimed in the Third Article of the declaration of rights in the new plan of government introduced among us; — for the reasons following, viz.:

"1. Because it asserts a right in the people to give away a power they never had themselves; for no man has a right to judge for others in religious matters; yet this Article would give the majority of each town and parish the exclusive right of covenanting for the rest with religious teachers, and so of excluding the minority from the liberty of choosing for themselves in that respect.

"2. Because this power is given entirely into the hands of men who vote only by virtue of *money* qualifications,* without any regard to the church of Christ.

"3. Because said Article contradicts itself; for it promises *equal* protection of all sects, with an exemption from any subordination of one religious denomination to another; when it is impossible for the majority of any community to govern in any affair, unless the minority are in subordination to them in that affair.

"4. Because by this Article the civil power is called to judge whether persons can conveniently and conscientiously attend upon any teacher within their reach, and oblige each one to support such teachers as may be contrary to his conscience; which is subversive of the unalienable rights of conscience.

"5. Because, as the convention say, 'power without any restraint is tyranny'; which they explain as meaning the union of the legislative, executive and judicial powers of government in the same hands; and it is evident that these powers are all united in the Legislature, who by this Article are empowered to compel both civil and religious societies to make what they shall judge to be *suitable provision* for religious teachers 'in all cases where such provision shall not be made voluntarily.'"

13. THOMAS JEFFERSON: "Truth can stand by itself" †

Despite the clause on the free exercise of religion in the Declaration of Rights in the Virginia Constitution of 1776, the Episcopal Church continued to receive support from the state in the form of land titles and other privileges. Thomas Jefferson and James Madison, therefore, led a prolonged battle in the Virginia legis-

* This refers to the property qualifications for voting in the Massachusetts Constitution.
† From Paul L. Ford (ed.), *The Writings of Thomas Jefferson* (New York, 1894), Vol. III, pp. 264–266, abridged.

*lature to bring about a complete disestablishment of the Episco-
pal Church. The bill for complete religious freedom proposed
by Jefferson and Madison finally became law in 1786. This law
included the notable words written by Jefferson: "no man shall
be compelled to . . . support any religious worship, place or
ministry whatsoever, nor shall be enforced, restrained, molested,
or burdened in his body or goods . . . but that all men shall be
free to profess, and by argument to maintain, their opinions in
matters of religion, and that the same shall in no wise diminish,
enlarge, or effect their civil capacities." In his book, entitled*
Notes on Virginia *(1785), we can read Jefferson's famous attack
on all attempts to coerce men in matters of religious belief. Read
the selection from the* Notes on Virginia *very carefully and try to
answer the following questions:*

1. Why does Jefferson oppose any attempt by the government to punish
   heresy or to compel a uniformity of belief?
2. What are the only practical means by which truth can be defended
   against error?

Truth can stand by itself. Subject opinion to coercion: whom
will you make your inquisitors? Fallible men; men governed by
bad passions, by private as well as public reasons. And why subject it to coercion? To produce uniformity. But is uniformity of
opinion desireable? No more than of face and stature. Introduce
the bed of Procrustes then, and as there is danger that the large
men may beat the small, make us all of a size, by lopping the
former and stretching the latter. Difference of opinion is advan-
tageous in religion. The several sects perform the office of a
Censor morum over each other. Is uniformity attainable? Millions
of innocent men, women and children, since the introduction of
Christianity, have been burnt, tortured, fined, imprisoned: yet
we have not advanced one inch towards uniformity. What has
been the effect of coercion? To make one half the world fools,
and the other half hypocrites. To support roguery and error all

over the earth. Let us reflect that it is inhabited by a thousand millions of people. That these profess probably a thousand different systems of religion. That ours is but one of that thousand. That if there be but one right, and ours that one, we should wish to see the 999 wandering sects gathered into the fold of truth. But against such a majority we cannot effect this by force. Reason and persuasion are the only practicable instruments. To make way for these, free inquiry must be indulged; and how can we wish others to indulge it while we refuse it ourselves. But every state, says an inquisitor, has established some religion. "No two, say I, have established the same." Is this a proof of the infallibility of establishments? Our sister states of Pennsylvania and New York, however, have long subsisted without any establishment at all. The experiment was new and doubtful when they made it. It has answered beyond conception. They flourish infinitely. Religion is well supported; of various kinds indeed, but all good enough; all sufficient to preserve peace and order; or if a sect arises whose tenets would subvert morals, good sense has fair play, and reasons and laughs it out of doors, without suffering the state to be troubled with it. They do not hang more malefactors than we do. They are not more disturbed with religious dissentions. On the contrary, their harmony is unparalleled, and can be ascribed to nothing but their unbounded tolerance, because there is no other circumstance in which they differ from every nation on earth. They have made the happy discovery, that the way to silence religious disputes, is to take no notice of them. Let us too give this experiment fair play, and get rid, while we may, of those tyrannical laws. It is true we are as yet secured against them by the spirit of the times. I doubt whether the people of this country would suffer an execution for heresy, or a three years imprisonment for not comprehending the mysteries of the trinity. But is the spirit of the people an infallible, a permanent reliance? Is it government? Is this the kind of protection we receive in return for the rights we give up? Besides, the spirit of the times may alter, will alter. Our rulers will become corrupt, our people careless. A single zealot may commence persecuter, and better men be his victims. It can never be too often repeated, that the time for fixing every essential right on a legal basis is while our rulers are honest, and ourselves united. From the conclusion of this war we shall be going down hill. It will not then be necessary to resort every moment to the people for support. They will be forgotten therefore, and their rights disregarded. They will forget themselves, but in the sole faculty of making money, and will never think of uniting to effect a due respect for their rights. The shackles, therefore, which shall not be knocked off at the conclusion of this war, will remain on us long, will be made heavier and heavier, till our rights shall revive or expire in a convulsion.

IN our final group of readings, we shall be examining some explanations of the American Revolution that have been written in the twentieth century by historians and social scientists. These selections will help us see how the ideas of conflict and consensus may be used to develop a historical interpretation of the American Revolution. All four of the writers in this section have read some of the same documents that are included in this volume and many others besides. Sometimes, they may even refer to some of the documents which you have just read.

The interpretations by these historians and social scientists are developed with the assumption that the reader already knows something about the events and the institutions of the Revolutionary period. Thus, as you read these selections, it would be well for you to remember what you already know about the historical events of the Revolutionary period as well as what you have learned about the problems of conflict and consensus from your reading of the previous selections in this volume. The following chronological list of events is included to help you refresh your historical memory.

1765 Delegates of the colonies except New Hampshire, Virginia, North Carolina, Georgia, meet to oppose the Stamp

Part 4

Some Explanations of the American Revolution By Twentieth Century Scholars

Act. First united effort to establish an extra-legal government to oppose England.

1774   "Intolerable Acts" passed in England; First Continental Congress meets in Philadelphia.

1775   Battle of Lexington-Concord.

1776   The Declaration of Independence adopted by the congress. Congress calls on all states to establish constitutions.

1777   Battle of Saratoga marks the turning point of the war. Articles of Confederation adopted by congress and sent to the states to be ratified.

1778   French Alliance signed. France enters the war. Virginia becomes the first major state to prohibit importation of slaves.

1780   Massachusetts adopts state constitution that includes a bill of rights and a distinct separation of powers. New York becomes the first state to cede its western lands to the Confederation. Pennsylvania starts a trend by gradually emancipating slaves.

1781   The Articles of Confederation given final ratification by all states.
Cornwallis surrenders at Yorktown.

1782   British forces withdraw from all southern ports and retain only a small force under Clinton in New York. Many Loyalists abandon property and move to England or other British colonies.
Commissioners meet in Paris to discuss peace terms.

1783   Treaty of Paris ends the war. Congress declares hostilities ended on April 19, eight years after the battle of Lexington and Concord.

1785   Jefferson's proposal for religious liberty accepted by the Virginia legislature.

1787   Shay's rebellion in Massachusetts. Land ordinance of 1787 provides for freedom of religion, trial by jury, permanently prohibits slavery in the Northwest territory.

14. VERNON LOUIS PARRINGTON: "Certain Social Consequences" *

Vernon Louis Parrington made a great contribution to the writing of American intellectual history. His Main Currents in American Thought *(Volumes I and II, 1927; and Volume III, 1930) are a landmark in the study of economic and social influences on the expression of ideas in American literature. In addition, Parrington believed that much of American history has been influenced by a conflict between opposing ideas and idealisms. Read the following selection from the first volume of Parrington's* Main Currents in American Thought *and consider the following questions:*

1. What does Parrington mean when he says that "a social war of classes followed upon hostilities against England"?
2. What class, in his opinion, came into a leading position in American life as a result of the American Revolution?

The swift crystallization of colonial sentiment in favor of republicanism, as the crisis developed, produced the American revolution of which John Adams wrote. The long leveling process of a hundred and forty years, with its psychology of decentralization, fruited naturally in a new political philosophy fitted to new-world conditions. Monarchy, with its social appanage of aristocracy, was a caste institution wholly unsuited to an unregimented America. The war brought this revolutionary fact home to the consciousness of thousands of colonials; and the liberalism that before had been vaguely instinctive quickly became eager and militant. The old order was passing; the day of the Tory in America was over for the present; the republican was henceforth

° From pp. 194–197, *Main Currents in American Thought,* Volume One, by Vernon Louis Parrington, copyright 1927 by Harcourt, Brace and World Inc.; renewed 1954, by Vernon Louis Parrington Jr., Louise P. Tucker, Elizabeth P. Tucker. Reprinted by permission of the publishers.

to be master of the new world. Out of this primary revolution
were to come other revolutions, social and economic, made possible by the new republican freedom.

The swift rise of a political philosophy traditionally regarded
as mean and traitorous was inexplicable to Tory gentlemen, and
aroused a fierce retaliatory opposition. A social war of the classes,
bitter, vindictive, followed upon hostilities against England. The
arrogance of the gentry during those brisk days when the new
spirit was rising is scarcely comprehensible to later Americans
unused to such frankness. The republicans were scorned by the
superior classes as unprincipled sedition-mongers, plotting treason against the King and society. If commoners flocked to town
meetings and outvoted the gentlemen, the latter were outraged
at the presumption of the "mobsters" in flouting their betters.
For the plain people to take things into their own hands was no
other than anarchy. The familiar records of the days are filled
with such aristocratic jests as this:

> Down at night a bricklayer or carpenter lies,
> Next sun a Lycurgus, a Solon doth rise.

"The dirty mob was all about me as I drove into town," said
Mistress Peggy Hutchinson, as she looked out on turbulent Boston
from her father's chariot; and her feminine contempt for the common people was an echo of the universal Tory contempt for republican mechanics and farmers. It was the duty of the vulgar,
as loyal subjects, to pay taxes and not lay them; to obey the law
and not make it. By far the most important consequence of the
Revolution was the striking down of this mounting aristocratic
spirit that was making rapid headway with the increase of wealth.
It sifted the American people as the migrations of the seventeenth
century had sifted the English people, keeping the republicans at
home and sending forth the Tories, weakening the influence of
the conservatives and increasing the influence of the liberals. Few
experiences in our history have proved so momentous in results
as this shift of power and change in personnel that resulted from

the great schism. A middle-class America was to rise on the ruins of the colonial aristocracy.

The unfortunate Loyalists were victims of their own blindness. They did not rightly estimate the driving power of the liberal forces released by the struggle, and failing to understand, they staked everything on the issue, and lost, and were driven rudely out of the land by the plebeian republicans whom they despised. The disruption of colonial society resulting from the expulsion of the Loyalists was far graver than we commonly assume. Shiploads of excellent gentlemen, and among them the most cultivated minds in America, were driven from their firesides and sent forth to seek new homes, whether in "Hell, Hull or Halifax" mattered little to the victors. Upward of forty thousand sought refuge in Canada; thousands more went to the Bahamas; and still other thousands returned to the old home. "There will scarcely be a village in England without some American dust in it, I believe, by the time we are all at rest," wrote the Loyalist Dutchman, Peter Van Schaak. Much suffering was endured and much bitterness engendered, and if for years the dominant temper in Canada was fiercely hostile to the United States, the mood is traceable to the expatriated gentlemen who transmitted to their children a grudge against the victorious republicans. It was an unhappy business, but it was scarcely avoidable once appeal was made to the sword. There was no longer place in America for the foolish dream of a colonial aristocracy.

The change of temper that came over American society with the loss of the Loyalists, was immense and far-reaching. For the first time the middle class was free to create a civilization after its own ideals. In rising to leadership it brought another spirit into every phase of life. Dignity and culture henceforth were to count for less and assertiveness for more. Ways became less leisurely, the social temper less urbane. The charm of the older aristocracy disappeared along with its indisputable evils. Although a few of the older wits like Mather Byles lingered on bitterly, and others like Gouverneur Morris accepted the situa-

tion philosophically, they belonged to the past. A franker evalua-
tion of success in terms of money began to obscure the older personal and family distinction. New men brought new ways and a
vulgar clamor of politics went hand in hand with business ex-
pansion. The demagogue and the speculator discovered a fruitful
field for their activities. The new capitalism lay on the horizon of
republican America, and the middle class was eager to hasten
its development. But a new economic order required a new political state, and as a necessary preliminary, the spirit of nationalism began that slow encroachment upon local frontiers which
was to modify profoundly the common psychology. Americanism
superseded colonialism, and with the new loyalty there developed
a conception of federal sovereignty, overriding all local authori-
ties, checking the movement of particularism, binding the separate commonwealths in a consolidating union. This marked the
turning point in American development; the checking of the long
movement of decentralization and the beginning of a counter
movement of centralization — the most revolutionary change in
three hundred years of American experience. The history of the
rise of the coercive state in America, with the ultimate arrest of
all centrifugal tendencies, was implicit in that momentous counter
movement.

15. MERRILL JENSEN: "The Problem of Interpretation" *

*Professor Merrill Jensen of the University of Wisconsin has writ-
ten a provocative analysis of the history of the Articles of Confederation. He is particularly concerned to relate the constitutional questions which were raised in the debates over the Articles
of Confederation to the political and social struggles of the
Revolutionary period. The following selection is a good example
of Professor Jensen's views about the "internal revolution" that*

° Reprinted with permission of the copyright owners, The Regents of the University of
Wisconsin, from pp. 6–15, 239, of Merrill Jensen, *The Articles of Confederation* (1959
edition), The University of Wisconsin Press.

took place in America during the revolt against Great Britain. Read this selection carefully and try to answer the following questions:

1. How does Jensen define the nature of the struggle that took place within America during the Revolution?
2. What kind of government and what kind of policies did the "radicals" want, according to Jensen?
3. What, according to Jensen, were the purposes of the "conservatives" in regard to the organization of the government for the Confederation?
4. Does Jensen's interpretation indicate that conflict was more important than consensus in the American Revolution?

The American Revolution was far more than a war between the colonies and Great Britain; it was also a struggle between those who enjoyed political privileges and those who did not. Yet the conclusions which may be drawn from the history of social conflict within the colonies and applied to such matters of mutual concern as the writing of a common constitution are seldom drawn and applied. Ordinarily the Revolution is treated as the end of one age and the beginning of another; a new country was born; political parties sprang into being; political leaders, full of wisdom learned during the Revolution, sought to save the new nation from the results of ignorance and inexperience. So runs the story.

But the story is true only in an external sense. The basic social forces in colonial life were not eliminated by the Declaration of Independence. There was no break in the underlying conflict between party and party representing fundamental divisions in American society. Those divisions had their roots in the very foundation of the colonies, and by the middle of the eighteenth century there had arisen broad social groupings based on economic and political conditions. More and more, wealth and political power were concentrated along the coast, in the hands of planters in the South and of merchants in the North. There were exceptions, of course, but by and large the colonial governments were in the hands of the economic upper classes. Exceedingly conscious of its local rights, the ruling aristocracy was willing to use democratic arguments to defeat the centralizing policies of Great Britain, but it had no intention of widening the base of political power within the colonies to accord with the conclusions which could be, and were, drawn from those arguments. On the contrary, it had kept itself in power through the use of a number of political weapons. As wealth accumulated and concentrated along the coast, as the frontier moved westward and became debtor and alien in character, and as the propertyless element in the colonial towns grew larger, the owners of property demanded "a political interpretation of their favored position" — that is, political supremacy — as a protection against the economic programs of debtor agrarians and the town poor. Encouraged by the British government, they gradually secured the political safeguards they demanded — property qualifications for participation in government and representation disproportionate to their numbers. The imposition of property qualifications for the suffrage and of even higher qualifications for office effectively quelled the political ambitions of the greater part of the town population, and the denial of proportional representation to the newly settled areas prevented the growing West from capturing control of colonial governments. Laws of entail and primogeniture insured the economic basis of colonial society, so much so that Thomas Jefferson believed that their abolition in Virginia would annul the privileges of an "aristocracy of wealth."

But the economic-political aristocracy which Jefferson hoped to abolish had not always been characteristic of the American colonies. In early Virginia and Maryland every free man, whether holding a property or not, could vote. The first serious attempt to impose a property qualification for the suffrage came with the Restoration and it met with bitter opposition. One of the significant acts of Bacon's Assembly in 1676 was the abolition of the property qualification imposed by the Berkeley regime. But the victory of the poorer elements was short-lived at best, and in Virginia, as elsewhere in the colonies by the end of the seventeenth century, the property qualification was an integral part of the political system. During the eighteenth century the tendency was in the direction of ever higher qualifications, and colonial assemblies continued to refuse adequate representation to the expanding West. By the middle of the century a small minority of the colonial population wielded economic and political powers which could not be taken from them by any legal means. This political oligarchy was able to ignore most of the popular demands, and when smoldering discontent did occasionally flare up in a violent outburst, it was forcibly suppressed. Thus democracy was decreasingly a characteristic of constitutional development in the American colonies.

Opposition to the oligarchical rule of the planters and merchants came from the agrarian and proletarian elements which formed the vast majority of the colonial population. Probably most of them were politically inert, but from their ranks nevertheless came some of the effective leadership and much of the support for revolutionary activity after 1763. In the towns the poorer people, although a small part of the colonial population, far outnumbered the large property-owners. Most of them — laborers, artisans, and small tradesmen — were dependent on the wealthy merchants, who ruled them economically and socially. Agrarian discontent, too, was the product of local developments: of exploitation by land speculators, "taxation without representation," and the denial of political privileges, economic benefits, and military assistance. The farmer's desire for internal revolution had already been violently expressed in Bacon's Rebellion and in the Regulator Movement, events widely separated in time but similar in cause and consequence.

To a large extent, then, the party of colonial radicalism was composed of the masses in the towns and on the frontier. In Charleston, Philadelphia, New York, and Boston the radical parties were the foundation of the revolutionary movement in their towns and colonies. It was they who provided the organization for uniting the dispersed farming population, which had not the means of organizing, but which was more than ready to act and which became the bulwark of the Revolution once it had started. Located at the center of things, the town radicals were able to seize upon issues as they arose and to spread propaganda by means of circular letters, committees of correspondence, and provincial congresses. They brought to a focus forces that would otherwise have spent themselves in sporadic outbursts easily suppressed by the established order.

Colonial radicalism did not become effective until after the French and Indian War. Then, fostered by economic depression and aided by the bungling policy of Great Britain and the desire of the local governing classes for independence within the empire, it became united in an effort to throw off its local and international bonds. The discontented were given an opportunity to express their discontent when the British government began to enforce restrictions upon the colonies after 1763. The colonial merchants used popular demonstrations to give point to their more orderly protests against such measures as the Stamp Act, and it was only a step from such riots, incited and controlled by the merchants, to the organization of radical parties bent on the redress of local grievances which were of far more concern to the masses than the more remote and less obvious effects of British policy. Furthermore, there arose, in each of the colonies, leaders of more than ordinary ability, men who were able to create issues when none were furnished by Great Britain, and who seized on British acts as heaven-sent opportunities to attack the local aristocracy — too strongly entrenched to be overthrown on purely local issues — under the guise of a patriotic defense of American liberties. Thus, used as tools at first, the masses were soon united under capable leadership in what became as much a war against the colonial aristocracy as a war for independence.

The American Revolution thus marks the ascendancy of the radicals of the colonies, for the first time effectively united. True, this radical ascendancy was of brief duration, but while it lasted an attempt was made to write democratic ideals and theories of government into the laws and constitutions of the American states. Fulfillment was not complete, for the past was strong and in some states the conservatives retained their power and even strengthened it. And once independence was won, the conservatives soon united in undoing, so far as they could, such political and economic democracy as had resulted from the war. Nevertheless it is significant that the attempt at democratization was made and that it was born of colonial conditions. The participation of the radicals in the creation of a common government is all-important, for they as well as the conservatives believed that a centralized government was essential to the maintenance of conservative rule. Naturally, the radicals who exercised so much power in 1776 refused to set up in the Articles of Confederation a government which would guarantee the position of the conservative interests they sought to remove from power.

The conservatives gradually became aware that internal revolution might be the result of continued disputes between themselves and Great Britain, but they were not agreed on the measures necessary to retain both "home rule" and the power to "rule at home." Some of them, like Joseph Galloway, sought to tighten the bonds between the colonies and the mother country and thus to consolidate the power and bulwark the position of the colonial aristocracy. Other conservatives, like John Dickinson, denied that Parliament had any authority over the colonies and cared little for a close tie with the mother country; what they demanded was a status that was in effect home rule within the British Empire. Complete independence was to be avoided if possible, for it was fraught with the danger of social revolution within the colonies. As these men became aware that conservative rule had as much or more to fear from the people of the colonies as from British restrictions, they sought more and more for reconciliation with the mother country, in spite of her obvious intention to enforce her laws by means of arms. But they made the fatal yet unavoidable error of uniting with the radicals in meeting force with force. They made themselves believe that it was neither traitorous nor illegal to resist with arms the British measures they disliked.

When independence could no longer be delayed, the conservatives were forced to choose between England and the United States. Some became "Tories," or "Loyalists." Others, the victims of circumstances partly of their own creation, fearfully and reluctantly became revolutionists. But in so doing they did not throw away their ideals of government. They were too cool, too well versed in checkmating radicalism and in administering governments in their own interest, to be misled by the democratic propaganda of the radicals. Not even John Adams, one of the few conservatives who worked for independence, was willing to stomach the ideas of Tom Paine when it came to the task of forming governments within the American colonies.

The continued presence of groups of conservatives in all the states, weakened though they were by the Revolution, is of profound importance in the constitutional history of the United States. They appeared in strength in the first Continental Congress. In it their ideas and desires were expressed. They were still powerful at the beginning of the second Continental Congress, but gradually their hold was weakened by the growing revolutionary movement in the various states. They were strong enough, however, to obstruct the radical program during 1775 and to delay a declaration of independence in 1776 until long after the radicals believed that independence was an accomplished fact. In the bitter controversies which occurred the conservatives stated their ideas of government. In its simplest form their objection to independence was that it involved internal revolution. When forced to accept independence, they demanded the creation of a central government which would be a bulwark against internal revolution, which would aid the merchant classes, which would control Western lands, which would, in short, be a "national" government. In this they were opposed by the radicals, who created a "federal" government in the Articles of Confederation and who resisted the efforts of the conservatives to shape the character of those Articles while they were in process of writing and ratification.

It is against such a background of internal conflict that the Articles of Confederation must be considered. Naturally any statement of the issues or principles of the Revolution, however broad the terminology, is likely to be misleading, for, as John Adams wrote, "the principles of the American Revolution may be said to have been as various as the thirteen states that went through it, and in some sense almost as diversified as the individuals who acted in it." There are inconsistencies and contradictions that cannot be forced into a logical pattern. Generalizations must therefore be understood as statements of tendencies and of presumed predominance rather than as unexceptionable statements of fact. Thus when the Revolution is interpreted . . . as predominantly an internal revolution carried on by the masses of the people against the local aristocracy, it is not without recognition of the fact that there were aristocratic revolutionists and proletarian loyalists; that probably the majority of the people were more or less indifferent to what was taking place; and that British policy after 1763 drove many conservatives into a war for independence.

Any interpretation of the American Revolution is subject to such qualifications, discomforting as it is to those who want complexities reduced to simple formulas. Any collection of facts must, however, be grouped around a theme, and particularly is this true of a movement having so many aspects as the American Revolution. Such grouping is unavoidable if one seeks to understand how the course of events, how the course of social revolution within the several states, often played a far more important role in determining political attitudes than did the more remote dangers of British policy.

In spite of the paradoxes involved one may still maintain that the Revolution was essentially, though relatively, a democratic movement within the thirteen American colonies, and that its significance for the political and constitutional history of the United States lay in its tendency to elevate the political and economic status of the majority of the people. . . .

The Articles of Confederation were the constitution of the United States from 1781 to 1789, when the Confederation Congress held its last session and turned over the government of the thirteen states to the new national government. The fact that the Articles of Confederation were supplanted by another constitution is no proof either of their success or of their failure. Any valid opinion as to the merits of the Articles must be based on a detailed and unbiased study of the confederation period. Though no such comprehensive study has yet been made, it is possible to draw certain tentative conclusions by approaching the history of the period from the point of view of the American Revolution within the American states rather than from the point of view that the Constitution of 1787 was a necessity, the only alternative to chaos.

An analysis of the disputes over the Articles of Confederation makes it plain that they were not the result of either ignorance or inexperience. On the contrary, they were a natural outcome of the revolutionary movement within the American colonies. The radical leaders of the opposition to Great Britain after 1765 had consistently denied the authority of any government superior to the legislatures of the several colonies. From 1774 on, the radicals continued to deny the authority of a superior legislature whether located across the seas or within the American states. The reiteration of the idea of the supremacy of the local legislatures, coupled with the social and psychological forces which led men to look upon "state sovereignty" as necessary to the attainment of the goals of the internal revolution, militated against the creation of such a centralized government as the conservative elements in American society desired. It can be said that the constitution which the radicals created, the Articles of Confederation, was a constitutional expression of the philosophy of the Declaration of Independence.

16. DANIEL BOORSTIN: "Some Peculiarities of Our Revolution" *

Professor Daniel Boorstin of the University of Chicago belongs to a recent generation of historians who have devoted a great deal of attention to studying the ideas and values that make up "the American way of life." To Boorstin and other historians like him, the most notable thing about American history is the absence of any sharply defined social conflicts of the kind that have taken place so often in European history. Extremist philosophies, Boorstin argues, do not succeed in America largely because the American consensus has been so powerful throughout our history. Read the following selection which Professor Boorstin has written about the American Revolution and consider the following questions:

1. What does Boorstin think is the most obvious peculiarity of our American Revolution?
2. What are the reasons that Boorstin emphasizes in explaining the conservative nature of our American Revolution?

The most obvious peculiarity of our American Revolution is that, in the modern European sense of the word, it was hardly a revolution at all. The Daughters of the American Revolution, who have been understandably sensitive on this subject, have always insisted in their literature that the American Revolution was no revolution but merely a colonial rebellion. The more I have looked into the subject, the more convinced I have become of the wisdom of their naiveté. "The social condition and the Constitution of the Americans are democratic," De Tocqueville observed about a hundred years ago. "But they have not had a

* Reprinted from pp. 68–75 of *The Genius of American Politics*, by Daniel Boorstin, by permission of The University of Chicago Press. Copyright 1953 by The University of Chicago Press.

democratic revolution." This fact is surely one of the most important of our history.

A number of historians (J. Franklin Jameson and Merrill Jensen, for example) have pointed out the ways in which a social revolution, including a redistribution of property, accompanied the American Revolution. These are facts which no student of the period should neglect. Yet it seems to me that these historians have by no means succeeded in showing that such changes were so basic and so far-reaching as actually in themselves to have established our national republican institutions. When we speak of the Revolution therefore, we are still fully justified in referring to something other than what Jameson's disciples mean by "the American Revolution as a social movement." If we consider the American Revolution in that sense, it would not be a great deal more notable than a number of other social movements in our history, such as Jacksonianism, populism, progressivism, and the New Deal. Moreover, in so far as the American Revolution was a social movement, it was not much to be distinguished from European revolutions; and the increasing emphasis on this aspect of our history is but another example of the attempt to assimilate our history to that of Europe.

The Revolution, as the birthday of our nation, must mean something very different from all this. It is the series of events by which we separated ourselves from the British Empire and acquired a national identity. Looking at our Revolution from this point of view, what are some features which distinguish it from the French Revolution of 1789 or the other revolutions to which western European nations trace their national identity? And, especially, what are those peculiarities which have affected the place of theory in our political life?

1. First, and most important, the United States was born in a *colonial* rebellion. Our national birth certificate is a Declaration of Independence, and not a Declaration of the Rights of Man. The vast significance of this simple fact is too often forgotten. Compared even with other colonial rebellions, the American

Revolution is notably lacking in cultural self-consciousness and in any passion for national unity. The more familiar type of colonial rebellion — like that which recently occurred in India — is one in which a subject people vindicates its local culture against foreign rulers. But the American Revolution had very little of this character. On the contrary, ours was one of the few conservative colonial rebellions of modern times.

We should recall several of the peculiar circumstances (most of them obvious) which had made this kind of revolution possible. At the time of the Revolution, the major part of the population of the American colonies was of British stock. Therefore, no plausible racial or national argument could be found for the superiority either of the inhabitants of the mother-country or of the continental American colonies. Even when Jefferson, in his *Notes on Virginia*, went to some trouble to refute Buffon and the Abbé Raynal and others who had argued that all races, including man, deteriorated on the American continent, he did not go so far as to say that the American races were distinctly superior.

Since the climate and topography of substantial parts of the American colonies were similar to those of the mother-country (and for a number of other reasons), there had been a pretty wholesale transplantation of British legal and political institutions to North America. Unlike the Spanish colonies in South America, which were to rebel, at least in part, because they had had so little home rule, the British colonies in North America were to rebel because, among other reasons, they had had so much. Finally, the North American continent was (except for sparse Indian settlements) empty of indigenous populations, hence barren of such local institutions and traditions as could have competed with what the colonists had brought with them.

All these facts were to make it easy, then, for the American Revolution to seem in the minds of most of its leaders an affirmation of the tradition of British institutions. The argument of the best theorists of the Revolution — perhaps we should call them lawyers rather than theorists — was not, on the whole, that America had institutions or a culture superior to that of the British. Rather their position, often misrepresented and sometimes simply forgotten, was that the British by their treatment of the American colonies were being untrue to the ancient spirit of their own institutions. The slogan "Taxation without Representation Is Tyranny" was clearly founded on a British assumption. As James Otis put it in his pamphlet, *The Rights of the British Colonies* (1764), he believed "that this [British] constitution is the most free one, and by far the best, now existing on earth: that by this constitution, every man in the dominions is a free man: that no parts of His Majesty's dominions can be taxed without their consent: that every part has a right to be represented in the supreme or some subordinate legislature: that the refusal of this would seem to be a contradiction in practice to the theory of the constitution."

According to their own account, then, the Americans were to have forced on them the need to defend the ancient British tradition; to be truer to the spirit of that tradition than George III and Lord North and Townshend knew how to be. They were fighting not so much to establish new rights as to preserve old ones: "for the preservation of our liberties . . . in defence of the freedom that is our birthright, and which we ever enjoyed till the late violation of it" (Declaration of Causes of Taking up Arms, July 6, 1775). From the colonists' point of view, until 1776 it was Parliament that had been revolutionary, by exercising a power for which there was no warrant in English constitutional precedent. The ablest defender of the Revolution — in fact, the greatest political theorist of the American Revolution — was also the great theorist of British conservatism, Edmund Burke.

2. Second, the American Revolution was *not* the product of a nationalistic spirit. We had no Bismarck or Cavour or any nationalist philosophy. We were singularly free from most of the philosophical baggage of modern nationalism.

Perhaps never was a new nation created with less enthusiasm. To read the history of our Revolution is to discover that the

United States was a kind of *pis aller*. This fact explains many of the difficulties encountered in conducting the Revolution and in framing a federal constitution. The original creation of a United States was the work of doubly reluctant men: men reluctant, both because of their local loyalties — to Virginia, Massachusetts, Rhode Island, and New York — and because of their imperial loyalty. The story of the "critical period" of American history, of the Articles of Confederation and the Constitution, tells of the gradual overcoming of this reluctance. It was overcome not by any widespread conversion to a nationalist theory — even the *Federalist* papers are conspicuously lacking in such a theory — but by gradual realization of the need for effective union.

In the period of the American Revolution we do discover a number of enthusiasms: for the safety and prosperity of Virginia or New York, for the cause of justice, for the rights of Englishmen. What is missing is anything that might be called widespread enthusiasm for the birth of a new nation: the United States of America. Until well into the nineteenth century, Jefferson — and he was not alone in this — was using the phrase "my country" to refer to his native state of Virginia.

3. Our Revolution was successful at the first try. This is equally true whether we consider it as a revolt against British rule or as a movement for republican federalism. There was no long-drawn-out agitation, no intellectual war of attrition, of the sort which breeds dogmas and intransigence. Thomas Paine's *Common Sense*, which is generally considered "the first important republican tract to be issued in America . . . the first to present cogent arguments for independence," did not appear until January 10, 1776. Down to within six months of the break, few would have considered independence; and even then the colonists had only quite specific complaints. There had been no considerable tradition in America either of revolt against British institutions or of republican theorizing.

The political objective of the Revolution, independence from British rule, was achieved by one relatively short continuous ef-

fort. More commonly in modern history (take, for example, the
European revolutions of the nineteenth century) any particular
revolt has been only one in a long series. Each episode, then, ends
on a note of suspense which comes from the feeling that the story
is "to be continued." Under those circumstances, challenges to
constituted authority follow one another, accumulating their ideo-
logical baggage.

In France, for example, 1789 was followed by 1830 and 1848
and 1870; a similar list could be made for Italy, Germany, and
perhaps Russia. Such repetition creates a distinctive revolutionary
tradition, with continued agitation keeping alive certain doctrines.
Repeated efforts provide the dogmatic raw material for a pro-
fusion of later political parties, each of which rallies under the
banner of one or another of the defeated revolutions or of a revolution yet to be made. But, properly speaking, 1776 had no sequel,
and needed none. The issue was separation, and separation was
accomplished.

17. BENJAMIN F. WRIGHT: "The Spirit of '76 Reconsidered" *

*Professor Benjamin F. Wright of the University of Texas is one of
America's foremost political scientists whose writings on American constitutional law have had considerable influence. The following selection is taken from a lecture given at Boston University on the general theme, "Consensus and Continuity, 1776–
1787." Read the selection very carefully and try to answer the
following questions:*

1. What, according to Wright, did the men of the Revolutionary era mean
   by their statements about equality?
2. What, in Wright's opinion, did the men of the Revolutionary era mean
   by "consent of the governed"?

* Reprinted with the permission of the Committee on the Gaspar G. Bacon Lectures
on the United States Constitution, from pp. 9, 13–20 of Benjamin F. Wright, *Consensus and Continuity, 1776–1787.* Copyright Boston University Press, 1958.

3. Does Wright think that the men of the Revolutionary era made any distinction between civil rights and property rights?
4. Does Wright think that there was a demonstrable consensus in the Revolutionary generation?

It is immensely significant of the Spirit of '76 and of the nature of American political thinking and action that these tiny and infant states should think it both natural and essential to have written constitutions as the basis for their governments, even when they were in a state of war. Rarely, if ever, did they debate the desirability of having a constitution. Rather they assumed that such documents were necessities. Their assumption can be understood only in terms of the long previous history of written constitutional documents in the colonies, and, in a somewhat different, but no less important sense in England. Beyond this background of history and experience, is the fact, which I pointed out some years ago, "that all of the literature of protest" in the years between 1761 and 1776 "has as its basic principle the conception of government under law." It was therefore only natural to the men of this time that, as John Adams tells us, as early as 1775 men's thoughts began to turn the problem of establishing the legal basis for new governments in place of those which were at least temporarily in abeyance. To the Americans it was not enough that there be revolutionary congresses or assemblies, though presumably representative of the patriotic citizens of the colonies. These representative bodies must govern in accordance with a known, settled, standing law. And from the first, and very temporary, constitutional document adopted by the Revolutionary Congress meeting at Exeter, New Hampshire in January, 1776 to the Constitution of Massachusetts, finally ratified and adopted in 1780, the evidence is clear and abundant that there was absolute consensus to the effect that a written constitution is a first essential of a free government.

Nearly all of the constitutions contained some statement about equality. The Virginia Constitution affirms that all men are by nature "equally free and independent." The Massachusetts provision (Article I of its Bill of Rights) asserts that "all men are born free and equal." It may here be observed that in no bill of rights, unless we include the frontier community of Vermont, which did not officially become a state until 1791, is the equality provision accompanied by the abolition of slavery. It seems evident that to most of the men of the Revolutionary era a declaration of equality did not run that far, any more than it included the principle that women should have equal legal rights with men or should share in the voting power. But in at least one state, Massachusetts, the Supreme Judicial Court held in 1783 that the provision concerning the equality of men had the legal effect of abolishing slavery, and slavery ceased to exist in that state from that day.

It is far from clear just what most of the men of '76 meant by equality, whether in the state bills of rights, or in the Declaration of Independence. Evidently they meant that Americans had equal rights with Englishmen. Most of them had a more ambitious, if rather vague, conception in mind: equality before the law, at least for free men; equality, that is, of legal rights, or equality in the power of asserting legal rights. It seems just as clear that few, if any, of the constitution makers had as simple a theory of equality as had Tom Paine, or one which was as sweeping and as inclusive.

Professor Elisha P. Douglass has argued, in his *Rebels and Democrats* (1955) that there were more egalitarians, in a sense which would have made them sharers in the point of view of Tom Paine, than has generally been recognized, though he of course concedes that these true democrats lost out except in Pennsylvania, and there the victory was not decisive nor enduring. To Professor Douglass the American Revolution would have been truly democratic if victory in the several states had resulted in the acceptance of simple majority rule, unicameralism, and complete equality of rights. In spite of his research and his cogent reasoning, there is little evidence that more than a few small groups of individuals favored anything approximating either economic equality or simple majority rule. Simple majority rule would not allow for the restraints on legislative action which became an increasingly important part of the American scene as an increasing proportion of adults came to have the vote. Nor is there reliable evidence that any large proportion of the population, or at least of that part which was articulate, favored a greater amount of social equality than that which was established during the Revolution.

For most men of that era equality did not have a nineteenth or twentieth century meaning. It is, for example, to be remembered that at the beginning of the Revolution there was a property qualification for voting in each of the colonies. At the end of the Revolution the property qualification remained except in four states where, for some or all offices, the payment of a public tax conferred the right of suffrage. In others the value of the property required had been reduced. A start had been made toward what was to become general, though not quite universal, in the first third of the nineteenth century, free adult male suffrage.

The consent of the governed is a conception and a principle which is as evident in most of these constitutions as it is in the Declaration of Independence. It is clear enough, however, from the fact that property or tax qualifications for voting are to be found in all of them, that the conception was ordinarily interpreted to mean the consent of those who have some property, and that may be the principal, though it is not necessarily the only, meaning to be given to the Virginia phrase "having sufficient evidence of permanent common interest with, and attachment to, the community." Women, children, and slaves would have no institutional means of expressing their consent.

The consent of the governed applies not only to the carrying on of public business from day to day and year to year, it applies most explicitly to the establishment of a constitution. Indeed, it applies to the establishment of society itself, and it is clear that many of the constitution makers of this time thought of themselves as taking part in the formation of a social compact. The usual criticism of the social compact theory, that it lacks historical authenticity, does not apply in America. The Mayflower Compact and the early plantation covenants were examples of this principle in action, and the state constitutions of the Revolution are, if anything, even more perfect illustrations of social compacts, since the people in the colonies reverted to a state of nature, to use the language popular in the eighteenth century, when they separated from England. They then established by agreement new political systems. The preamble of the Massachusetts Constitution of 1780 is worth quoting on this point: "The body politic is formed by a voluntary association of individuals: It is a social compact by which the whole people covenants with each citizen and each citizen with the whole people that all shall be governed by certain laws for the common good." A clearer and more emphatic statement of the social compact theory is probably not to be found elsewhere in equally condensed form.

Guarantees of civil liberties are to be found in all of the Revolutionary bills of rights, and also in those constitutions of that period which contain no separate bill or declaration of rights. These guarantees are, for the most part, in the direct line of succession from the bills and petitions of rights which form so notable a part of English history in the seventeenth century, many of which trace their ancestry to Magna Charta. The phrase translated from Magna Charta, "the law of the land," is more commonly found than the one which later becomes generally adopted in American constitutions, due process of law. The guarantees vary somewhat, but they generally include the rights of habeas corpus, of trial by jury in certain circumstances, usually a jury of the neighborhood or vicinity, of bail, of a free trial in open court. Frequently freedom of the press is included, in some freedom of religion also appears. The right to assemble and petition or remonstrate is found in most of the longer bills of rights; this is both an inheritance from England and a right which the colonial leaders had very recently employed — or been denied. The right of suffrage for all is not included among the natural or legal rights of men guaranteed in the bills of rights. But it is also to be noticed that the tendency toward liberalizing the qualifications for voting were such that only one state, South Carolina, had a religious qualification for voting by the end of this period. Only the Delaware Constitution prohibits the slave trade.

One of the somewhat surprising provisions encountered in these early bills of rights is what amounts to the right of revolution, even as against the government established under the Constitution, when the government fails to provide that freedom and security for which it was established. Thus the Virginia Constitution, after specifying the objectives of government, stipulates that "when any government shall be found inadequate or contrary to these purposes, a majority of the community hath an indubitable, unalienable and indefeasible right to reform, alter or abolish it, in such manner as shall be judged most conducive to the public weal."

If one reads that statement out of context, it can easily be taken as a doctrine of simple majority rule, as though Tom Paine rather than George Mason were the author of the Virginia Constitution. Such an interpretation is erroneous, partly because the spirit of the Virginia Constitution includes most explicitly the protection of minority rights, partly because of the suffrage limitations, partly because this constitution like all except one or two of those of the Revolution, provides for a system of separation of governmental powers. Indeed, it provides in two places for a separation of powers. The Declaration of Rights stipulates "that the legislative and executive powers of the state should be separate and distinct from the judiciary." The body of the Constitution provides that "the legislative, executive, and judiciary departments shall be separate and distinct, so that neither exercise the powers properly belonging to the other." This is almost as extreme a statement of the separation of powers as that written by John Adams, supported by an overwhelming vote of the citizens of Massachusetts in the town meetings, and ratified into the

constitution of 1780. The final article in the Massachusetts Bill
of Rights reads:

"In the government of this commonwealth, the legislative department shall never exercise the executive and judicial powers,
or either of them: The executive shall never exercise the legislative and judicial powers, or either of them: The judicial shall
never exercise the legislative and executive powers, or either of
them: to the end it may be a government of laws, and not of
men."

It is surely one of the most striking facts in the institutional and
philosophical history of the United States that the legislative-exec-
utive quarrels during the colonial period convinced the colonists
of the desirability of a separation of powers rather than a union
of powers. They had experienced more of separation and of
checks and balances than was consistent with even moderately
satisfactory government. Of course, they quickly abandoned the
worst feature of the colonial system — the admixture of local and
external control — but they continued to desire as much of separation as was compatible with the selection of the executive within
the colony. It took just one year of constitution making in the
states to develop the principle that the governor should be elected
by the voters. In the first state constitutions the executive (in all
of them except Pennsylvania a single executive) was elected by
the legislative body or by one house of the legislature. But in
1777 New York adopted the constitution drafted originally by
John Jay, later Chief Justice of the United States, which provided
for a governor elected by popular vote. The example of New
York was followed by Massachusetts in 1780, by New Hampshire
in 1784 and, sooner or later, by all other states.

Some historians have seemed to find that the separation of
powers was not the true expression of the point of view of the
Revolution, primarily, if I understand their arguments, because
the first group of constitutions had a less effective separation between executive and legislative bodies than the later ones, and
in several of the early constitutions the upper house of the legis-

lature was elected by the lower, as were the judges of higher state courts in some states. It seems to me that, considering the history of colonial governments and the controversies between governors and councils appointed by the Crown or by the proprietors and the elected lower houses, they provided for an astonishing amount of separation and of checks and balances in the very first constitutions. In the next group of constitutions, Georgia's alone excepted, there was a more effective separation of powers. The constitutions of Massachusetts and New Hampshire, adopted in 1780 and 1784, both of which were drafted by bodies elected especially for the purpose and both ratified only after popular vote in town meetings, contained the greatest separation of powers and checks and balances of any of the documents of the time.

In various ways, then, all of these constitutions give evidence of a sceptical view of human nature, of a distrust of popularly elected legislative and executive agents; none comes near to vesting as much unrestricted authority in government as does the French Declaration of Rights of Man and of the Citizen, written in 1789. There one finds, after two articles which are reminiscent of the American bills of rights, the statement (Article III) that all sovereignty is in the nation, and a subsequent statement (Article VI) that "law is an expression of the general will." This is, from the point of view of the American principles accepted during the Revolution, much nearer to being totalitarian than to being pluralistic. The only limitation upon the expression of power seems to be the will of the nation, which is to say, the law of the national legislative body. The only effective restriction, other than the power of the suffrage would seem to be revolution. To the Americans of '76, '77 and '80 such doctrine was dangerous to liberty and the rule of law.

There is one other provision found in nearly all of the bills of rights of the Revolutionary era, one which I have intentionally left to the end, the right of property. Article one of the Virginia Declaration of Rights provides that the rights of citizens include "the means of acquiring and possessing property." Article one of the Massachusetts Bill of Rights, immediately after reference to life and liberty, guarantees the right "of acquiring, possessing, and protecting property." The three together add up to — "In fine, that [right] of seeking and obtaining their happiness and safety." To these authors of our first bills of rights, who were also leaders of the American Revolution, there was no thought of a conflict between civil rights on the one hand and property rights on the other. The right to acquire, possess, and be protected in the possession of, property was one of the most important of all civil rights. The conception of a conflict between civil and property rights is a development of the nineteenth century.

The thesis of this lecture has been that the political ideas of the American Revolution, the Spirit of '76, is not accurately represented by Tom Paine nor adequately by the Declaration of Independence. For that spirit is also to be found in the state constitutions of 1776, or 1777 and of 1780, constitutions which were, in many instances, written by the men who wrote and signed the Declaration of Independence.

To the men of this time there was no contradiction between the libertarian ideals of the Declaration of Independence and the limitations or restrictions of the state constitution. Contrary to what Charles Merriam and others have said, the age was immensely constructive, not merely destructive. The constitutions were essential to the attainment and protection of the rights asserted in the Declaration of Independence and also of those asserted in the state bills of rights. The leaders of '76 wanted protection and security for their liberties, and, to their way of thinking, protection was unattainable without a written constitution. They wanted order and stability as well as liberty, and to most of them order meant legal order. To them the ancient dilemma, liberty *or* stability, individual rights *or* authority was easily solved, for it was no dilemma at all. They believed that true authority was based upon liberty, and liberty required constitutional order.

These state constitutions were the most advanced, by far the most democratic, constitutions in the world at that time, but they were not documents of the kind which would have been acceptable to Tom Paine, or at least none except the atypical, and short lived constitution of Pennsylvania. That constitution provided, except for the strange mechanism of a Council of Censors, more reminiscent of Plato's *Laws* than of anything in the American experience, a relatively simple and almost majoritarian system. But even the Pennsylvania Constitution of 1776, one which was unpopular in that state almost from the first month of its establishment, contained constitutional restrictions upon the power of the legislative body and guarantees of individual rights.

The extent to which the various men and colonies demonstrated a consensus on political and constitutional principles is amazing, unless one realizes that they were drawing upon the reservoir supplied partly by the central stream of English development from Magna Charta to the Bills of Rights, but even more by the experience of self-government in the colonies. One can find some points of difference, even a few relatively peculiar features among the documents, including the constitutions, but the differences are slight indeed when one compares these constitutions with the forms and accepted principles of government in Europe, even in the mother country, England. . . .

Now that you have completed the readings in this volume, a good way for you to organize what you have learned is to write a paper on this final question:

> **Do you think that there was a deep-seated political and social conflict among Americans who supported the American Revolution, or was this a period in which there was a remarkable consensus on political and social questions?**

Be sure to defend your explanation with as much specific historical evidence as possible. If you wish to write a longer research paper on this problem, the following books would be helpful.

I. Source Materials, Writings, Biographies

Samuel Eliot Morison, *Sources and Documents Illustrating the American Revolution*. 1948.

George E. Peek, *The Political Writings of John Adams*. 1954.

Carl Van Doren, *Benjamin Franklin*. 1939.

Edward Dumbauld, *The Political Writings of Thomas Jefferson*. 1953.

Richard M. Dorson, *American Rebels: Narratives of the Patriots*. 1953.

II. Historical Interpretations of the Revolutionary Period

Part 5

Conclusion

John F. Jameson, *The American Revolution Considered as a Social Movement*. 1960.

Edmund Morgan, *The Birth of the Republic 1763–1789*. 1956.

Merrill Jensen, *The New Nation*. 1950.

Elisha P. Douglass, *Rebels and Democrats*. 1955.

Esmond Wright, *Fabric of Freedom 1763–1800*. 1961.

John C. Miller, *The Triumph of Freedom*. 1948.

3 4 5 6 7 8 9 0